Education and
Poverty

Recent Titles in
Contributions to the Study of Education

Education and Poverty

EFFECTIVE SCHOOLING IN THE UNITED STATES AND CUBA

Maurice R. Berube

CONTRIBUTIONS TO THE STUDY OF EDUCATION, NUMBER 13

GREENWOOD PRESS

Westport, Connecticut
London, England

21073.3   371.96
                 B 552

Library of Congress Cataloging in Publication Data

Berube, Maurice R.
  Education and poverty.

  (Contributions to the study of education, ISSN 0196-
707X ; no. 13)
  Bibliography: p.
  Includes index.
  1. Socially handicapped children—Education—Case
studies. 2. Education—United States—Case studies.
3. Education—Cuba—Case studies. I. Title. II. Series.
LC4069.B47 1984   371.96'7   83-26428
ISBN 0-313-23468-X (lib. bdg.)

Library of Congress Catalog Card Number: 83–26428
ISBN: 0-313-23468-X
ISSN: 0196–707X

First published in 1984

Greenwood Press
A division of Congressional Information Service, Inc.
88 Post Road West, Westport, Connecticut 06881

Printed in the United States of America

10 9 8 7 6 5 4 3 2 1

To the memory of my mother, Medora Berube, 1904–1943

CONTENTS

PREFACE

The original thesis of this book was to investigate how different political and social systems educate a poor population, especially in urban centers. The model for the book was Urie Bronfenbrenner's *Two Worlds of Childhood: U.S. and USSR.* I assumed that I could compare approaches to effective education of the urban poor in the United States with those used in a socialist system that had a similar constituency and possibly similar problems. Cuba was selected as the socialist country because of its success with its Literacy Campaign shortly after the Revolution, and because one-third of its population is black, (a racial composition that compares with that of the United States). I felt that investigations of other socialist educational systems, such as in the Republic of China or the Soviet Union, would not have as much pertinence because of the lack of a black population.

That thesis has had to be altered. My visit to Cuba in May 1983 indicated that in very few instances could Cuba and the United States be compared on equal terms. While Bronfenbrenner's study of Soviet and American education found the two powers rather equal in their economic development, Cuba can best be compared with other Latin American countries rather than with the United States. Cuba is still a poor and underdeveloped country whose main income derives from agricultural products—sugar and tobacco—whereas the United States is a highly industrialized and developed country. This fact was made clear to me in myriad ways. In education, the very lack of classroom supplies compared with the abundance in a United States classroom was painfully obvious.

Nevertheless, the basic concept of investigating the effective schools movement in the United States and the educational system in an underdeveloped country still remained sound. The relationship between education and poverty can be further explored by two case studies: the effective schools movement in a First World country, the United States, and that of a Third World country, Cuba. Cuba has not only had success in educating its poor through its much heralded Literacy Campaign in 1961, but it is also fast creating a school system sufficiently effective to place Cuban education in the category of developed nation. As my Cuban hosts were quick to point out, some aspects of social life in Cuba are already characteristic of developed nations in a society that still is economically underdeveloped. Such is the case with the Cuban health system; the major causes of death are now those of a developed country. In short, the basic concept of the book remains valid, even though the perspective and focus have changed somewhat.

I want to thank the Cuban Ministry of Education for allowing me to conduct my study of Cuban education. My original suggestion of visiting primary and secondary schools, collecting research data, and interviewing specific key education officials was adhered to. With the exception of two schools mentioned in Karen Wald's *Children of Che* that I requested to visit and which were no longer in operation, my every wish was honored. Moreover, I found in my discussions with education officials that past and present problems were described as frankly as accomplishments. In his study of the Literacy Campaign, Jonathan Kozol observed that officials of the Ministry of Education were quite open and that they felt there was nothing to hide. My experience corroborates that view.

I am indebted to a number of individuals who were instrumental in the preparation of this manuscript. In Cuba, I would like to mention the work of my interpreter, Juan Jacomino, who was tireless in his efforts in translation. Mr. Jacomino, a

twenty-six-year-old man who speaks three languages fluently
(Spanish, English, and Swahili), is a prime example of the gains
of the Cuban Revolution. The son of a *campesino*, Mr. Jacomino would not have had the opportunity to study languages
had it not been for the Revolution. Merida Lopez, researcher
with the Ministry of Education, was my faithful guide through
the intricacies of Cuban education. I should also like to thank
Antonio Mosot, director of Extra School Activities; Magaly
García Ojeda, director of Primary Education; and Elisa Wong
García, deputy minister of Education. Most important, I want
to thank José R. Fernández, minister of education, who gave
of his valuable time so willingly. Mr. Fernández, a hero of
the Revolution who had been jailed by Battista, consented to
a final interview at the end of my trip that placed Cuban education in context. And I am indebted to Oscar Lorenzo of
the Cuban Ministry of Foreign Affairs who was a constant
companion and was able to expedite formalities. Instrumental to the manuscript was Jonathan Kozol's strong recommendation to the Cuban government that I be allowed to conduct
my study. Mr. Kozol, who figures prominently in this book,
based that recommendation chiefly on his admiration for my
earlier books on community control. I appreciate his key role.

In the United States, I am grateful to three individuals at
Old Dominion University who were able to fund my trip to
Cuba. They were Bruce Anderson, chairman of the Depart-
ment of Educational Leadership and Services; Ulysses Van
Spiva, dean of the Darden School of Education; and David
Hagar, acting academic vice-president. In addition, Carlton
Brown of Old Dominion University read key parts of the
manuscript and offered critical advice. My son, Michael Berube, rendered a useful task as proofreader. The staff of the
Center for Cuban Studies was particularly helpful. Special
mention must be made of the diligence and thoroughness of
my copy editor, Abby Levine. And finally I am beholden to
the students in my graduate seminars on whom some of the
ideas in the manuscript were tested.

PART
ONE: Effective Schools in the
United States

1
EDUCATION IN THE UNITED STATES: AN OVERVIEW

In the past generation, a new myth about schooling in America has emerged. That myth has proclaimed that the poor are, by and large, uneducable. It has been espoused by radical and conservative educational critics alike, by the academic community, by schoolteachers in charge of these children, and by the public. It is an uncompromising myth based on incomplete social data and the day-to-day difficulty of educationally reaching a largely black and minority poor in the urban schools of America. It is, unfortunately, a false myth.

That this myth has flourished is understandable. Middle-class teachers despaired of the progress of their urban minority pupils. Concerned with a lower-class life-style that depreciated education, they were susceptible to the myth of the uneducable poor. Socially concerned academics sought to show that the poor fail in the public schools—and failed in the past—not because of innate ethnic cultural deficiencies but because of the lack of sufficient economic background. Their intentions were good: They did not want to interpret the failure of the urban black and minority poor in terms of an inherent genetic or cultural inferiority. Nonetheless, their economic interpretation, despite its sophistication, created an easy scapegoat.

Teacher spokesmen faced a dilemma in explaining educational success and failure. On the one hand, teachers and their representatives were quick to point out that educational failure often was due to causes beyond the classroom: in short, the home and family background. For example, Dave Darland, associate director of the National Education Association in charge of instruction and professional development, could brand the movement for teacher accountability of the 1970s "oversimplistic." One should not, he cautioned, "hold individual teachers totally responsible for educational outcomes." Rather, one should merely consider their "efforts."[1]

On the other hand, teachers and their representatives are quick to accept praise for their success. Albert Shanker, president of the New York City teachers' union local (as well as the national union), welcomed the news of a rise in reading scores among New York City pupils, including students who are poor. He told the press that "it's very good news" and that "we owe much to the teachers who worked so hard under very tough conditions."[2] Shanker was all too typical of many teachers who accept praise for the success of their students but have been hesitant to accept blame in the past for declining reading scores.

My aim is not to show attitudinal inconsistencies among teachers regarding the mysteries of teaching and learning. But it is crucial to note that the concept of social background has been deeply embedded in the psyche of many teachers as an all-too-ready excuse for the academic failures of children who are poor.

Perhaps the classic statement on the inability of the poor to succeed in school (or anywhere else) was expressed by Harvard political scientist Edward Banfield. In his now famous *The Unheavenly City*, written in 1970, Banfield states that most social problems are insoluble because they depend on changing one's psychology, or culture of poverty, which he believes government is incapable of doing. "Lower class poverty" he writes, "is 'inwardly' caused" (by psychological inability to provide for the future, and all that this inability implies)."[3] Critics were quick to point out that this was armchair sociology. Empirical studies, such as that conducted by Eliot Liebow (*Tally's Corner*), indicate that it is not lack of willingness among the poor to advance themselves as much as lack of opportunity and training.

Nevertheless, Banfield is adamant. Schooling for the poor is unnecessary because the poor lack the ability.

The answer is that the children who are stimulated into mobility in school are ones whose initial class culture permits or encourages—perhaps even demands—mobility. The more nearly upper class the child's initial culture, the more susceptible he is to being "set in motion" by the school. At the other end of the continuum, the lower class child's culture does not even recognize—much less value—the possibility of rising or, rather, of doing those things, all of which require some sacrifice of present for future gratification, without which rising is impossible.[4]

Banfield's solution for the poor in school is quite simple: Let them leave school. As for the poor in society, he is equally blunt: The best hope for eliminating poverty is to have the poor die out.

It is instructive that Banfield's work was highly touted, appearing in excerpts in national magazines and introduced to the Nixon presidential cabinet by urban affairs advisor Daniel Moynihan.

There were those who persevered in the notion that the poor were educable. They observed the testimony of individual poor boys and girls who obtained a modicum of social and economic success through the public schools and colleges. They believed that despite the overwhelming failure of the black and minority poor in the nation's schools, some students who were poor succeeded. That is not to say that one refuses to confront the depressing fact that a large majority of our nation's students who are poor fail in the schools. But many believe that there is still hope.

For the past two decades, the debate over inner-city schools has revolved around where to place the blame for the educational failure of urban youth. Minority parents and other critics have charged that the public schools—specifically the administrators and teachers—are at fault. One educational journalist, Nat Hentoff, entitled one of his books *Does Anybody Give a Damn?*. These advocates suggested that the school system must be changed to suit the needs of a new clientele.

They infused spirit into the educational reform movement of the sixties.

On the other hand, many educators have pointed to the home as the major influence. Disadvantaged families produce low student motivation, cultural deprivation, and poor home reinforcement. For the past decade and a half, the research has overwhelmingly supported this view. However, recent research is mounting indicating that some schools have had success in educating an urban poor. Such impressive reports cut against the grain of studies that maintain family background is the main influence in a student's educational achievements. These "new optimists" show that some of the urban poor have been effectively taught.

The aim of this book, then, is to investigate these scattered reports, some major, some minor—and to draw a profile of what makes for sound and effective schooling for an urban poor. Its overriding goal is to first establish that some of the poor succeed in public and private schools and then investigate the implications for public educational policy in America. As a corollary, it is necessary to draw a comparison with what socialist countries are achieving in this respect, especially those socialist systems, such as Cuba, which have a black urban constituency. In the preface to La Vida, Oscar Lewis provocatively suggests that socialist countries are free from a culture of poverty.[5] If that be the case, it would be instructive to discover what these systems are doing.

One must avoid simplification. Whereas the doctrine that the poor are, by and large, uneducable, is an extreme position, we must avoid the contrary that all poor students can surmount their backgrounds. There is massive evidence surrounding us daily—as well as in the past—that the poor have severe disadvantages because of background that hamper them from success in school. Nevertheless, it is going to extremes to suggest that schools have little impact on the lives of the poor.

The facts are clear. The large majority of poor urban students fail each year. They are behind in reading achievement by some two or more years. In New York City, for example, 53.7 percent are below their expected grade level in reading.[6] In the ghettoes of New York City that amount increases from two-thirds to three-quarters.[7] A study by Professor Daniel U. Levine and his associates in seven major cities (Chicago, Cleveland, Cincinnati, Houston, Los Angeles, St. Louis, and Kansas City, Missouri) analyzes the relationship between poverty and low achievement scores. Levine correlated low reading achievement not only with poverty but with a high *concentration* of poor people within the city. This made him conclude that for most urban classrooms, there is an "overload" factor whereby once the problems "reach certain threshold points in severity and frequency, the institution tends to operate ineffectively and/or dysfunctionally."[8] Levine errs in solely measuring child inputs and ignoring school resources. Nonetheless, poor children, for the most part, fail in urban classrooms.

In 1960, the respected Harvard psychologist, Jerome Bruner, ushered in a decade of school reform with a proclamation of utmost optimism. "We begin with the hypothesis that any subject can be taught effectively in some intellectually honest form to any child at any stage of development. . . . Considerable evidence is being amassed that supports it."[9] A decade later, that optimism would be severely challenged as large-scale failure was revealed in urban schools. At present, however, there is mounting evidence that teachers and administrators in some schools have had a measure of success in educating those most recalcitrant—the urban poor, mostly black and minority.

It was not until the middle sixties that the question of educating an urban poor came to a climax. Civil rights groups pressured city school systems to make public standardized reading test scores. The disclosure of widespread failure unleashed a flood of criticism indicting the public school system. A school reform movement resulted—itself an offshoot of the civil rights movement—that criticized the operation of American public schools and recommended a host of innovations from the ungraded classroom to community control of urban schools.

That criticism of the schools has been aptly called Romantic. Such critics as Jonathan Kozol, Herbert Kohl, Paul Good-

man, and Nat Hentoff had as their working assumption the
belief that urban public schools had performed adequately in
the past. The failure of public schools to educate a largely new
black poor was attributed to the malfeasance of many teachers and administrators. Had not Bruner declared that every
child was educable?

The Romantics were deadly serious about the conse-
quences of miseducation. Jonathan Kozol entitled his book,
Death at an Early Age, with the equally provocative subtitle,
*The Destruction of the Hearts and Minds of Negro Children
in the Boston Public Schools*; Nat Hentoff called his book *Our
Children Are Dying*; and Charles Silberman originally entitled *Crisis in the Classroom, Murder in the Classroom*. The
theme of an intellectual and spiritual death as well as an end
to economic opportunity and social mobility was clearly struck
by the Romantics. And indicating that the public was attuned
to the importance of the schools, Kozol won the prestigious
National Book Award in 1968 for his *Death at an Early Age*.

These books were for the most part front-line accounts. Kozol and Kohl were teachers in public schools. Kozol shows how
the racism of fellow teachers in a Boston public school accounted for the defeat of the black youngsters there. Kohl was
a teacher in a Harlem school who was able to raise the educational level of his students through nontraditional methods
such as a creative writing program. Both Hentoff and Silberman were journalists who spent much time in the schools they
wrote about.

The Romantics reached a height in popularity by the end
of the 1960s with the publication of Charles Silberman's *Crisis in the Classroom*. Silberman's account had been given the
imprimatur of a $300,000 Carnegie Foundation grant to study
teaching in America. He went beyond that mandate to investigate the conditions of the public school in a report that became a best-seller.

What Silberman found was that these public schools were
"joyless." They were failing the child. He struck the Romantics' theme that the schools had the potential to do better.

It is not unreasonable, however, in a society that prizes (or claims to
prize) equality of opportunity, to expect schools to be a *significant*

influence—to expect them to make the opportunities open to their students less dependent on their social origins. And that means making it possible for students from every social class and every ethnic and racial group to acquire the necessary basic skills.[10]

Proceeding from Bruner's dictum that all children were educable, Silberman accused the schools of failing in that task. His remedy was educational innovation, specifically the Open School Method. Silberman had concluded that schools fail "because of mindlessness" rather than "maliciousness."[11] Most important, he believed there was no need for protest movements to restructure education—the politics of educational reform could simply come about by wishing it. Silberman eschewed the confrontation politics that has been the hallmark of most educational reform in the sixties as well as most of social reform throughout our history. Nevertheless, he gave strength to the Romantics' vision of better schooling for all.

What has happened since Bruner and the Romantics' declaration of optimism was essentially the publication in 1966 of James Coleman's massive study *Equality of Educational Opportunity*.[12] Commissioned by the federal government in order to ascertain the degree of school integration under the 1964 Civil Rights Act, the study went beyond its narrow mandate. Coleman and his colleagues set out to find out among some 645,000 elementary students who learned and why. There were difficulties at the outset. Few school administrators in large cities cooperated with Coleman. Nonetheless, the scale of the study was impressive, making it the second largest social science study behind Gunnar Myrdal's classic study of race in America, *An American Dilemma*. The Coleman Report, as it came to be known, had a definitive ring to it.

Coleman and his associates concluded that family background was the chief determinant of educational achievement. (There was a contradictory finding that students with a sure sense of destiny and control of their fates, whether black or poor, performed adequately academically.) For the most part, however, Coleman found that socioeconomic background was the whole story in learning. Schools and their resources were said to have little effect.

Coleman's study did not initially receive the serious attention it deserved for political reasons. The study had been interpreted as a call for greater efforts at school integration since socioeconomically mixed students (white middle-class pupils and black poor pupils) seemed to perform well. As a result, the Johnson administration sought to minimize the report's impact by issuing it close to July 4, 1966, when most Americans including top journalists, were vacationing. A few scattered mentions of the Coleman study were made in the fall (including one by myself), but it did not receive more attention until three years later when Christopher Jencks "rediscovered" the report in the pages of the prestigious *New York Times* magazine.[13] But the Romantics still held court, and it was not until the early 1970s, when Jencks reanalyzed the data for his 1972 study *Inequality*, that Coleman's influence was strongly felt in intellectual and academic circles.[14]

The Coleman Report attempted to measure school resources—such as teacher qualifications, libraries, laboratories, and curriculum—as an influence on pupil achievement. When the researchers found that there was practically no relation between school resources and educational achievement, they concluded that differences in achievement level had to be attributed to what the student brought to school. As a consequence, they correlated parental education with student achievement, leading them to the proposal that home environment was the most important ingredient in achievement. Although Coleman and his colleagues proceeded from the assumption that black schools were inferior in resources, they found that black schools' resources were relatively equal to those of white schools.

Of the six ethnic/racial groups surveyed by the Coleman Report, only Oriental Americans recorded some measure of academic success. Black Americans fall behind the longer they are in school. Most important, the disparity begins in the first grade, reinforcing the belief that educational achievement is dependent on family background.[15]

The Coleman Report is a cross-sectional study based on questionnaires dealing with one point in time. It was criticized for several serious methodological flaws. First, the sample could lead to a bias since most teachers and principals did not respond; 70 percent of high schools, 75 percent of elementary schools; and several large city school systems did not cooperate. Second, the study is based on a standardized verbal achievement test in terms of outcome for educational achievement. This does not measure other characteristics of a school's influence such as those affecting motivation, pupil adjustment, and behavior. Third, the study is limited because it is not longitudinal. And last, the measure of school characteristics—school resources—is more quantitative than qualitative in nature. It does not measure school climate, teacher and principal expectations, and behavior, all of which are crucial to learning.

Nonetheless, advocates of the Coleman Report perceived it as no less than the "most important effort of its kind ever undertaken by the United States government."[16] This raised serious policy implications for the schools. Supporters of the Coleman study felt that little could be done in terms of reforming the schools. Instead, they thought of a "social strategy designed to increase the incomes of lower-class families by raising occupational levels or wage rates, by tax exemptions or income supplementation . . . [instead of] . . . direct spending on schools.[17]

In *Inequality*, a reworking of the Coleman data, Jencks begins with the proposition that Americans believe in educational opportunity. From that point he examines the school reform movement of the 1960s and finds it wanting. Those reforms failed, he charges, because they sought to solve only symptoms, not causes. The basic assumption of the Great Society, Jencks maintains, was that education was the best mechanism for breaking the vicious cycle of poverty. Indeed, President Johnson, a former schoolteacher imbued with the rhetoric of education, believed that education could solve the problems of the world.[18]

Jencks demurs from that view. His research suggests that school resources have little effect on the *quality* of education. Jencks concludes that economic success seems to depend more on luck and on-the-job competence, more on personality than on technical skills. In his later book, *Who Gets Ahead*, he adds emphasis to the amount of schooling one obtains as a chief factor in occupational success.

There were a number of false starts with Jencks's approach. First, his reading of educational history was askew. The school reform movement did not fail because of inner shortcomings; rather, it failed because of strong opposition and underfinancing. Various groups, from teacher organizations to community organizations, thwarted the move toward community control and integration, for example. And the increasing demands of the escalating war in Vietnam ensured that federal efforts were not sufficiently funded to make a serious attempt at compensatory education. Moreover, later studies, such as Head Start, showed these compensatory education efforts to be more successful than was originally thought by such as Jencks.

With the exception of a few (myself, Colin Greer, and black educators Kenneth Clark and Ron Edmonds), Jencks's work was highly praised. One indication of its nearly universal acceptance was the quick publication of a companion piece, *The Inequality Controversy*, edited by Donald Levine and Mary Jo Bane (the latter co-author of *Inequality*). This book contains not a single article critical of Jencks.

In *Inequality*, backed by a three-year, half-million-dollar Carnegie Foundation grant, Jencks and his colleagues reinterpret the Coleman Report, drawing on the Blau and Duncan study of occupational structure.[19] Jencks concludes that learning is dependent on one's socioeconomic background and that occupational success is as dependent on luck as on any other factor. That latter speculation was chided by Colin Greer as a "Lady Bountiful" approach and by myself as reviving the Horatio Alger myth. Like Coleman, Jencks believes that a school's resources have little effect on achievement since the greater influence is home background. Although many teachers and administrators would agree with Jencks's diagnosis of achievement, they would disagree that schooling has as little importance as he seems to give it.

Jencks advises that equality in America had best be sought through some form of income redistribution as mobility through the schools is no longer possible for the poor. And he subtly changes the direction of the debate of how best to provide equality in American life by shifting the focus from equality of opportunity to equality of results.

One critic of Coleman and Jencks examines adults—that segment of the population that was not observed by traditional studies—and asks how education can be made more lasting. In the early seventies, Herbert H. Hyman and his associates undertook a study published as *The Enduring Effects of Education*.[20] Their investigation is unique and interesting in several aspects. For one thing, Hyman et al. point out that in all previous studies, only the young were incorporated into the research; the major works on the effectiveness of education never attempted to trace how long or how much the effect of education endured into adulthood.

As Hyman shows, the Coleman Report refers only to a population of children enrolled in specified elementary and high school grades in 1965. The major question investigated in the Coleman study is whether variations in the resources of schools made a difference in cognitive accomplishments of pupils or whether individual differences in knowledge among pupils were better explained by other factors, such as personal or family background.

As for Jencks's *Inequality*, Hyman perceives that Jencks examined the adult population only in terms of economic status and position as opposed to knowledge. Jencks was primarily concerned with eliminating inequality, and status is not the same as knowledge.

Hyman and his associates use an innovative research methodology called *secondary analysis* in their study of the enduring effects of education. They extracted data from the files of the Gallup poll, the National Opinion Research Center at the University of Chicago, and the Survey Research Center at the University of Michigan. A total of fifty-four surveys, each designed to be an unbiased sample of the white adult population at the time, was used. Because of possible confounds with nonwhite birth cohorts in the earlier data, nonwhites were excluded in this study (they were to be included in later studies when Hyman's methodology was refined). Data were collected from eighty-thousand birth cohorts and spanned the years from 1949 to 1971. Persons included ranged in age from over twenty-five to under seventy and represented various educational levels.

Hyman reports his "findings established that the better educated have wider and deeper knowledge not only of bookish facts, but also of many aspects of the contemporary world; that the differences override obstructions and endure despite aging and characterized individuals who represent several generations and several historical periods in the functioning of schools."[21] Repeatedly, Hyman outlines the purpose of education as to prepare individuals for a lifetime of learning by equipping them with motivation, an intellectual outlook, and skills to continue to learn. Hyman firmly concludes: "Many and varied measurements of thousands of adults drawn from a long series of national samples and thus representing students taught in all of the nation's schools and colleges over a long period, lead us to conclude that education produces large pervasive and enduring effects on knowledge and receptivity to knowledge.[22]

Another extensive study (that has received little attention) is the Senate's report on education. The United States Senate established the Select Committee on Equal Educational Opportunity in February 1970 to study the effectiveness of existing laws and policies assuring equality of educational opportunity. The committee was chaired by then senator Walter Mondale. After three years and testimony from hundreds of students, teachers, parents, administrators, educational experts, and government officials, the committee produced a thirteen-thousand-page report on equal educational opportunity in the public schools.[23]

Equal educational opportunity, as used by the committee, was defined to be both the results of education and the way those results were produced. As to the results of education, the consensus of the Senate committee was that schools do make a difference in a child's life. As part of its exhaustive investigation, the committee addressed the question of the Coleman Report and concurred that full educational opportunity was denied to millions of American children who were born poor or nonwhite; however, in the same statement, it emphasized the impact of education as fundamental to success in American life. If the public schools were ineffective, then lack of educational opportunity to the poor and non-white would be insignificant and a moot point.

The question of the success or failure of the public schools cannot be answered lightly. There are too many factors to be considered for us to examine one aspect of the schools and then dismiss the issue with finality, as did Coleman and Jencks. It is much too simplistic to dismiss the schools as failures based upon the arguments of these critics. Furthermore, it is illogical and invalid to examine components of the schools and society unrelated to the goals of education and use them as an attack against the public schools.

What is necessary is research such as Hyman's and the Senate investigation. Examination of the schools must be based upon the goals of education and must include not only the current school population, but those who have passed through the system into adulthood. Only by basing research on these goals of education and taking into consideration the adult population can we make valid conclusions about the success or failure of the public schools.

Nevertheless, the prevailing orthodoxy in educational circles is that educational achievement is controlled by socioeconomic factors. Coleman and Jencks have won the day. Most teachers, administrators, and parents would consider social class to be the most important ingredient in the educational recipe. However, we shall discover that a good number of the poor have succeeded in public school in the past, and that there are some schools where learning takes place regardless of social class backgrounds.

Notes

1. Dave Darland, "Some Complexities of Accountability," *Today's Education* (January-February 1975), p. 21.

2. Albert Shanker, "Extra Effort Shows in Reading Results," *New York Times,* June 14, 1981, p. E7.

3. Edward Banfield, *The Unheavenly City* (Boston: Little, Brown, 1970), p. 126.

4. Ibid., p. 141.

5. Oscar Lewis, *La Vida* (New York: Random House, 1966), p. xlix.

6. New York City Public Schools, *Pupil Reading Achievement* (New York: Board of Education, 1980), p. 20.

7. Ibid.

8. Daniel U. Levine, "Concentrated Poverty and Reading Achievement," *The Urban Review* 11, no. 2 (Summer 1979), p. 77.

9. Jerome Bruner, *The Process of Education* (New York: Vintage Books, 1960), p. 33.

10. Charles Silberman, *Crisis in the Classroom* (New York: Random House, 1970), p. 62.

11. Ibid., p. 81.

12. James Coleman et al., *Equality of Educational Opportunity* (Washington, D.C.: U.S. Government Printing Office, 1966).

13. Christopher Jencks, "Reappraisal of the Most Controversial Educational Document of our Time," *New York Times* magazine, August 1969.

14. Christopher Jencks et al., *Inequality* (New York: Basic Books, 1972).

15. Frederick Mosteller and Daniel P. Moynihan, eds., *On Equality of Educational Opportunity* (New York: Random House, 1972), p. 21.

16. Ibid., p. 4.

17. Ibid., p. 50.

18. Maurice R. Berube, "Education and the Poor," *Commonweal* (March 31, 1967), p. 46.

19. Peter M. Blau and Otis Dudley Duncan, *The American Occupational Structure* (New York: John Wiley and Sons, 1967).

20. Herbert N. Hyman et al., *The Enduring Effects of Education* (Chicago: University of Chicago Press, 1975).

21. Ibid., p. 58.

22. Ibid., p. 109.

23. Francesco Cordasco, ed., *Toward Equal Educational Opportunity: The Report of the Committee on Equal Educational Opportunities, U.S. Senate* (Montclair, N.J.: Montclair State College, AMS Press Inc., 1974).

2
EARLY AMERICAN SCHOOLS AND THE URBAN POOR

What has been the historical record in educating an urban poor? If we can ascertain the lessons of the past, perhaps we can prescribe for the future. Unfortunately, there are no clear indications concerning the performance of the poor in urban schools. What strong evidence exists mainly concerns the great immigration era at the turn of the century and shows that a majority in the early decades of the twentieth century failed in schools. However, that evidence is subject to scrutiny. For one thing, most immigrants from the Eastern European countries had a language barrier that disappeared over time, and subsequently their performance in school improved. For another, jobs—especially unskilled—were plentiful; this provided incentive to students with problems to leave school. In the final analysis, it is a question of whether one perceives the glass as half full or half empty. The dominant historical school, known as Revisionists, perceive the glass to be half empty. But we do know that a sizeable number of the poor succeeded in school.

The Revisionists are so-called because of their tendency to "revise" the myths and misconceptions of traditional educational history. They are new educational historians who grew up in the socially minded 1960s and their concern is with a more politically conscious educational history. These young academics include the historians Michael Katz, Colin Greer, and Joel Spring and the economists Samuel Bowles and Herbert Gintis.

The Revisionists maintain that the public school was basically an agent of social control with the specified purpose of keeping the poor in their place. Nineteenth-century campaigns to organize and maintain public schools more often than not were morality campaigns in order to keep the poor God-fearing and clean above all else. The underlying assumption of the Revisionists is that the public schools have never adapted to educating an urban poor and that if the teachers and administrators could adapt, urban schooling would be more effective. In this regard, the Revisionists tend to believe that reform is possible. There are some exceptions to these views; Bowles and Gintis, for example, hold that reform is not possible unless the entire structure of political and economic life takes a socialistic turn.

The Immigrants

A key work is Colin Greer's *The Great School Legend*, published in 1972. Greer shows that the overwhelming majority of immigrants failed in urban public schools. He attempts to explode "the great school legend"—that the schools were wholly the equalizer of the conditions of man, as Horace Mann and many of his disciples envisioned them to be. And Greer holds to the belief that educators have the capacity to do better and that it is now time "we finally take our traditional rhetoric seriously."[1]

Greer's main investigations involved regular surveys in five major cities—New York, Chicago, Philadelphia, Detroit, and Boston—as well as some smaller cities and occasional surveys in five other major cities. He found that "no more than 60 percent" of students were at grade level in these classrooms.[2] This led him to conclude:

From 1890 on, so far as quantitative evidence allows us to document, the schools failed to perform up to their own claims of anywhere near the popular definition of their role. In virtually every study undertaken since that made of the Chicago schools in 1898, more

children have failed in school than have succeeded, both in abso-
lute and relative terms. As schools expanded to match the growth of
cities, so urban decay and school failure became virtually synony-
mous clarion calls among reformers and Jeremiahs alike.[3]

Moreover, the pattern continues. "Today still," Greer writes,
"more than 40 percent of our school children are permitted
to fail."[4] The difference is that the ethnic groups have changed,
from Jews, Irish, and Italians to blacks, Puerto Ricans, and
Mexicans.

The work of Michael Katz is the most provocative. Katz
found that the public schools in the past had been *in effect*,
agents of social control: They operated to keep the poor in
their place. Rather than become avenues of social mobility,
Katz argues, the public schools merely maintained the status
quo. He is clear on this point: "Despite the existence of free,
universal, and compulsory schooling, most poor children become poor adults. Schools are not the great democratic engines for identifying talent and matching it with opportunity.
The children of the affluent by and large take the best marks
and the best jobs."[5] And Katz attributes that result to the in-
tentional aim of school leaders. The inability to provide mobility for the poor "cannot be explained either by genetics or
by theories of cultural deprivation: it is the historical result
of the combination of purpose and structure that has characterized American education for roughly the last hundred
years."[6]

Like Greer, Katz believes in the possibilities of the schools
despite their poor performance for over a century. He maintains that "the time has come" for serious educational reform.
That reform, however, must entail a radical restructuring of
educational forms. Katz agreed with the leaders of the community control/decentralization movement that centered in
New York in the late 1960s. He hoped that such control would
shift power to teachers and students as well as to local communities.

The Revisionists exaggerate the lack of social mobility in
America. They emphasize statistics showing an economic
system that has remained virtually unchanged in distribution

of wealth since the end of World War II, citing studies showing that there was little mobility in nineteenth-century America. In her book *The Revisionists Revised*, Diane Ravitch (a
conservative educational historian) scores this weakness of the
Revisionists' analysis. She points out that the most important
historical findings have been those of social historian Stephan Thernstrom, who found in *The Other Bostonians* marked
social mobility in Boston in the years 1880–1970. *Poverty and
Progress*, Thernstrom's earlier study of Newburyport, Massa-
chusetts, during the years 1850–1880, revealed few mobility
patterns. However, the Boston years showed mobility at a time
when the Industrial Revolution was in full force. Ravitch also
notes that the 1962 landmark Blau and Duncan study (which
figures so heavily in Jencks's *Inequality*) concludes that there
is a large amount of upward mobility in the American occupational structure.[7] The Blau-Duncan study was based on a
national sample of twenty-thousand men.

Michael Katz, perhaps the most thoughtful of the Revisionists, disputes Ravitch's critique. He characterizes her approach as being wedded to the notion that "progress can be
continued through a steady application of the democratic-
liberal tradition of reform. . . ."[8] Katz feels that Ravitch was
not sufficiently sophisticated in her understanding of the Revisionists' work. According to Katz, the school system has
helped: "the well-to-do better than the poor and by and large,
helps to reproduce rather than alter the class structure. That
argument does not deny that substantial amounts of individual mobility have always taken place.[9]

How one perceives the mobility that has taken place is, then,
a matter of degree. Nevertheless, the various spokesmen have
drawn the widest implications from these interpretations. Some
of the Revisionists, like Katz, wish for structural educational
reform; others look toward income redistribution and away
from school reform. The neoconservatives, such as Ravitch,
satisfied with the past and present, want to see the status quo
preserved.

Nonetheless, some ethnic groups—notably the Jews,
Chinese, and Japanese—were able to *adapt* to the public
school more readily than others. This suggests that the cul-

tural values and characteristics of these groups enabled them to perceive the schools as a means of social mobility. Professor Nathan Glazer has suggested three reasons for social mobility of ethnic groups: 1. cultural strengths; 2. economic needs; and 3. ethnic and racial discrimination.[10] Although it appears that a blend of all three factors does in fact operate, the historical evidence is rather clear that racial discrimination and economic fluctuations have affected blacks adversely. On the other hand, strong cultural patterns and economic vicissitudes have affected all ethnic groups. Stephen Steinberg, for example, argues in *The Ethnic Myth* that immigrant Jews at the turn of the century had a head start in the economic race because they were nearly all skilled tradesmen.[11]

Successes: The Jews—A Case Study

Let us analyze more closely the case of the Jews since their rise has been spectacular and quite heralded. More has been written about the Jewish experience—and more is being written—than about that of any other ethnic group. This is partially explained by the strong intellectual tradition in the American Jewish community. Certainly, as Stephen Steinberg has pointed out in *The Academic Melting Pot*, Jews are overrepresented in intellectual and academic pursuits in relation to their numbers in the society.[12] That alone is an indication of the obsession with education in the Jewish community. The cultural passion for education among Jews is undisputed; it is perhaps the most distinguishing characteristic of that group in America. And that passion became manifest and persisted during early immigrant days at the turn of the century.

Consider the testimony of the *Jewish Daily Forward*, which served as a beacon and gentle prodder during those early years of the twentieth century. The *Forward* was constantly reminding its readers about the value of education. The performance of Jewish immigrant children impressed many teachers. One told the *Forward's* editor that "all the teachers are amazed by the [the Jewish children's] ability. . . . The best minds in each class are Jewish. . . . The children show the

greatest interest in their studies."[13] The Jewish immigrants'
passion for education is also illustrated by their early view toward sports. The *Forward* exhorted its readers to concentrate
on education and pay little attention to games. "The Irish boys
want to be boxers," the *Forward* editorial reads, "and the
Jews—debaters."[14] Jews adapted more readily to city schools
than did other immigrant groups.

Greer claims that Jews were the least "retarded" (not in the
grade for their age level) of all city school students. A study
for the U.S. Immigration Commission in 1908 showed that over
40 percent of all students in twelve major cities were retarded.[15] In Boston, that figure was only 6 percent for Ger-
man Jews, while Jews were less retarded in Chicago and New
York than other nationalities, including native Americans.[16] A
government report in 1901 in New York City observed that
"the city college is practically filled with Jewish pupils . . .
[and] . . . in the lower schools, Jewish children are the de-
light of their teachers for cleverness. . . ."[17] By the twenties
and thirties, more than half of New York City doctors, lawyers, dentists, and public school teachers were Jewish. By
1935, the Detroit school system could report that 70 percent
of Jewish youth had graduated from high school, compared to
40 percent of all other groups.[18]

It cannot be argued that Jews tended to perform better academically because of strong family structure. Italians, who
were perhaps the most family-minded, did not do nearly so
well. Nor could social class account for the difference between these two groups, even though more Jewish immigrants were skilled than Italians. Two historians who have
carefully examined the evidence conclude that ethnic cultural values were responsible so that" Russian-Jewish culture
prepared that group to fare well in terms of educational success, and that Southern Italians' culture was at odds with the
demands of formal schooling in America."[19]

These investigators found throughout the historical literature that Jews put primacy on education. And most important, Jews perceived their new land to be one of untold opportunity where talent and hard work translated to success.
Southern Italians, on the other hand, placed emphasis wholly

on close familial ties and distrusted "outside" institutions. This meant a negative attitude toward schooling, which was seen as an agency of the upper class for manipulation.

These cultural differences suggest the complex nature of education and poverty. If we were to consider school achievement simply to be a function of social class, we could be seriously misled. In the same fashion, if we perceive school achievement as independent of differing ethnic cultures, we could also make a significant error.

Other historians—not Revisionists—have argued that the performance of the Jews, Japanese, and Chinese in the public schools was a result of these groups *first* improving their income and *second* achieving educational success. The work of Selma Berrol, Thomas Kessner, and Sherry Gorelick adduces evidence to that view. Berrol's article "Education and Economic Mobility: The Jewish Experience in New York City, 1880–1920" is the key document.

These historians make a number of crucial points: 1. that the percentage of poor Jews who went on to a free city college in New York was small; 2. that most poor Jews did not go on to any college in those years; and 3. that Jews became mostly white collar by the 1920s and then sent their children to a free university system in New York in large numbers in the 1930s. Indeed, Berrol shows that by 1923, approximately 11 percent of city college graduates—who numbered no more than two-hundred—could be identified as poor Jews.[20] Only by the 1930s were there large enough numbers of Jews in the city colleges to provide significant statistics. Thomas Kessner found that 57 percent of Jews were in the white-collar class in 1925 as compared with 64 percent in 1934.[21] Berrol concludes that Jewish "widespread use of higher education is mostly a third generation phenomenon made possible by the economic security earned by other non-educational routes."[22]

The image of Jewish students graduating from New York's city colleges en masse is only partly true. According to Sherry Gorelick in *City College and The Jewish Poor*, Jews *did* predominate in the city colleges. At the turn of the century, fully three-quarters attending City College were Eastern European Jews (poor Jews), and by 1919, 78 percent were Jewish.

At Hunter College, Eastern European Jews comprised 8 percent of the student body about 1900 and by 1919 were 38.7 percent.[23] But these statistics are deceiving. Higher education was not yet a mass enterprise. That came with time and especially the initiative of the GI Bill of Rights after World War II. As a consequence, these percentages translate into small numbers. CCNY had only 209 students graduating in 1913, of which Eastern European Jews accounted for 23. The proportion of those graduating was less than those attending. At Hunter, only 58 women were Eastern European Jews out of an urban Jewish population of nearly a million.[24] Although Jewish students "achieved more success than many other youngsters," they constituted a "selected few."

What can we conclude? It is clear that *some* Jews—a goodly number—achieved in public schools at the turn of the century and after. It is a case of perceiving the glass partially filled with water. Historians such as the Revisionists and Berrol and Kessner prefer to see the glass as mostly empty. Let us review the evidence from a different perspective.

1. *A substantially large number of poor Jews succeeded in school.* Colin Greer determined that over 60 percent of these Jews in public schools in Boston, Chicago, Detroit, Philadelphia, Pittsburgh, and New York failed at the time of the great immigration. That would leave some 40 percent who were able to achieve in public schools—a substantial figure, not to be lightly disregarded. Moreover, Selma Berrol cites two studies conducted in 1909 and 1920 indicating that "in general, Jewish children were doing well in school."[25] She also says that Jews found New York schools "different from anything the immigrants had known."[26] They were free and nonsectarian. New York City also had free colleges. These factors played a large part in the educational consciousness of a group whose "cultural capital" included "an awareness that education could be a worthwhile investment."[27]

2. *Jews moved so rapidly into the white-collar class during the early decades of the twentieth century because of their success in public schools.* Although it is true that only a select few Jews attended city colleges at the turn of the century (despite being the dominant group at those schools), their en-

try into white-collar occupations was due to their ability to
perform well in public schools. Berrol notes that "East European Jews used formal education more than other immigrant groups . . . [and] it was only one of the many reasons
for the rapid and significant upward mobility experienced by
the New York East European Jewish Community."[28] Kessner
adds that Jews were "clearly advantaged by their pursuit of
American education, they qualified in far larger numbers than
their parents or than Italian offspring as professionals, clerical and technical personnel, managers and officials."[29]

3. *When Jews began attending free city colleges in the 1930s
in great numbers, many were poor.* Kessner shows that "relatively more Jews kept their jobs" in the depression because
they were, as white-collar workers, least affected.[30] Nonetheless, a substantial number of Jews were out of work. In New
York, 47 percent of the unemployed were in either white-
collar or skilled job classifications that most Jews held. In addition, Gorelick cites a New York State legislative study in
1944 that found students of the 1920s and 1930s to come
"largely from lower income groups" whose homes showed a
"continuous and severe struggle for existence" and where a
great majority worked summers and even during the school
year although tuition was free.[31] Moreover, there is the testimony of many Jewish autobiographies citing the authors'
poverty when attending the free city colleges. In conclusion,
many poor Jews succeeded in public school due to their strong
cultural penchant for education and their ability to adapt to
their environment.

There is also a suggestion that the Catholic poor did well
in parochial schools. Although very little research has been
done on Catholic schools, *The Education of Catholic Americans*, the monumental study of Catholics and their schools
conducted in the mid-sixties by Andrew Greeley and Peter
Rossi, shows that Catholic school graduates rose to occupy a
high economic level in our society. Nevertheless, more research on achievement of both public and Catholic schools is
essential.

The Revisionists and subsequent historians performed a
useful task in deflating previous rhetoric that inflated the ca-

pacities of the public schools. These institutions were not the engines for wholesale social mobility in our society as they had been portrayed to be. On the other hand, it was not true that only a few were able to use the schools as a way out of poverty.

Individual Case Studies

Finally, one must not overlook the testimonies of those born in poverty who were able to rise above it with the help of their schooling. They provide dramatic evidence that some can make it, and they cut across racial and ethnic lines.

Perhaps the most eloquent testimony of a poor boy who achieved mobility through the schools is that of the literary critic Alfred Kazin. In a moving memoir, A *Walker in the City*, Kazin recalls the aspirations and fears of failure of young Jews in a Brownsville, New York, ghetto of the 1930s: "I miss all those ratty little wooden tenements, born with the smell of damp in them, in which there grew up how many school teachers, city accountants, rabbis, cancer specialists, functionaries of the revolution, and strongarm men for Murder, Inc."[32]

His particular family background was one of poverty during the Great Depression. His father was a house painter who was only able to obtain work intermittently. Kazin movingly describes his family's plight:

I can still hear my mother's anxious question each time my father returned from the labor pool in front of the Municipal Bank—*Geyst arbeten?* Will there be work this week? From the early thirties on, my father could never be sure in advance of a week's work. Even the "long" jobs never seemed to last very long, and if he was on an "outside" job, a rainy day was a day lost. It puzzled me greatly when I came to read in books that Jews are a shrewd people particularly given to commerce and banking, for all the Jews I knew had managed to be an exception to that rule. I grew up with the belief that the natural condition of a Jew was to be a propertyless worker like my painter father and my dressmaker mother and my dressmaker uncles and cousins in Brownsville—workers, kin to all the workers of the world, dependent entirely on the work of their hands. All happiness in our house was measured by the length of a job.[33]

Alfred, the first-born American of his family, became their hope. He was expected to "shine" for them and to "redeem" their existence. Consequently, he approached the school with fear. It was the place where he would have to "succeed, to get ahead of the others in the daily struggle. . . ."[34] Kazin went on to City College and then wrote his critically acclaimed study of American literature, *On Native Ground*, in 1942. He successfully pursued an academic and literary career.

Another who "made it" is the editor for the past twenty years of the influential journal of opinion *Commentary*, published by the American Jewish Committee. Norman Podhoretz made "one of the longest journeys in the world" from "Brooklyn to Manhattan—or at least from certain neighborhoods in Brooklyn to certain parts of Manhattan."[35] Although Podhoretz is reluctant to discuss his family in detail in his autobiography *Making It*, he describes his childhood in Brownsville as belonging to a class where he and "everyone I knew were stamped as inferior: we were in the *lower* class."[36] Podhoretz's father was a milkman whose weekly salary of sixty dollars in the forties placed him among the working poor. Podhoretz was, in essence, according to his teacher and mentor, a "filthy slum child."[37] He would have remained so if not for a certain English teacher in high school, unidentified in his memoirs, "who decided that I was a gem in the rough."[38] Throughout these high school years, this teacher was determined that Podhoretz win a Harvard scholarship so that he would not "wind up with all the other horrible little Jewboys in the gutter (by which she meant Brooklyn College)."[39] She monitored his development and took him often to Manhattan to museums, restaurants, and the more opulent world of Fifth Avenue.

Podhoretz succeeded. He won the Harvard scholarship, but because it was not large enough to cover expenses and his family could not make up the difference, he had to forgo it. He was saved from the "gutter" of Brooklyn College, however, by a full scholarship with additional stipend to Columbia. At Columbia, he distinguished himself academically and went on to win a fellowship at Cambridge University.

Podhoretz's fascination with class led him, after a number

of revulsions at the liberal direction the nation was taking in the 1960s, to a position as a leading neoconservative editor and writer. *Commentary*, along with *The Public Interest*, became the focal point of neoconservative thought in the early 1970s. (Neoconservatives can be described as a brand of conservatives who were formerly liberals and leftists.) Paradoxically, Podhoretz now adheres to the theory that social class is the chief influence in school and society.

One unique neoconservative promoted a myth about his early poverty. Daniel Patrick Moynihan, the senator from New York and a former Harvard professor, promulgated a Lincolnesque tale about his youth and poverty while holding to the doctrine that social class determined everything about educational achievement. Moynihan would hark back to his days as a shoeshine boy on Times Square and as a longshoreman living in the tenements of Hell's Kitchen in New York City. Although encouraging this account of his early life, Moynihan, according to one commentator, reached an intellectual turning point with the publication of the Coleman Report "which, in Moynihan's view, challenged virtually every assumption that had been made about the role of public education in American life. . . ."[40]

Moynihan's version of his early years is part truth. For about three or four years prior to high school, he was plunged into poverty when his journalist father abandoned the family. But his mother remarried, and he also spent time with his maternal grandfather, a successful attorney. Eventually his mother bought a saloon. Moynihan was born to the middle class, and except for a brief sojourn among the poor, remained within that class. Nevertheless, he preferred to cite his poverty years as a focal point to show how far he had come. It is ironic that his great intellectual influence, the Coleman Report, stresses family background as contributing to achievement in school.

One route that has been open to many poor youngsters has been athletic scholarships to college. Dick Gregory, the comedian and black rights activist, is a case in point. Gregory's family was on welfare during his youth in the 1930s and 1940s; his father had abandoned the family. Gregory distinguished himself in high school in St. Louis on the track team. His first motivation to get on the team was when he learned that members showered in the gym in the afternoons. By his senior year, he was deluged with scholarships despite mediocre grades, and he seriously considered attending college. He chose Southern Illinois in Carbondale and attended for two years before being drafted into military service in 1954. In his memoir, Gregory recalls his early poverty as a time when he was not poor, "just broke." He explains that "poor is a state of mind you never grow out of, but being broke is just a temporary condition."[41]

For the student who was poor and attained mediocre grades, athletic scholarships were perhaps one avenue to higher education. Many students obtained a college education in this fashion. Land-grant colleges and the free municipal colleges in New York City, however, maintained sub-rosa policies of open admissions. For the poor in New York, admissions requirements increased until the open admissions policy was publicly declared in 1970.

The most dramatic story of a poor boy who made good—through use of the schools—may be that of Claude Brown. Brown was reared in poverty in Harlem: His father never made more than sixty dollars a week even in the fifties and sixties, drank heavily, and beat Claude. Brown was an early gang member participating in various small crimes—one of which was continually skipping school. In the end, no Manhattan school would admit him. He was sent to the Wiltwyck School for disturbed children at age eleven and stayed there two years. He became friendly with Ernest Papanek, Wiltwyck's director, who had high hopes that young Claude, with his quick mind, would become a success. His parents held no such high expectations. Brown's climb to success was not in a straight line. After Wiltwyck, he returned to his Harlem gang. He was shot in the stomach at age thirteen in an attempted robbery and was sent to reform school. After leaving reform school, Brown gradually outgrew his Harlem companions and environment. He moved to middle-class Greenwich Village and attended night school while working. In the mid-sixties, he graduated from Howard University, wrote a remarkable memoir—*Manchild in the Promised Land*—and then graduated from Rutgers University Law School.[42]

Another example is that of Mary E. Mebane, now a professor at the University of Wisconsin-Milwaukee. Mary grew up as a young black girl in relative poverty in North Carolina during the Great Depression. She was "part of the last generation born into a world of total legal segregation in the Southern United States."[43] Her mother worked as a factory hand in a tobacco plant and her father, a poor dirt farmer and junkman, died when Mary was in high school.

Mebane became interested in the world of books in the second grade when she first heard the story of the Ugly Duckling read to her by a black schoolteacher. Her interest in school was discouraged by her parents. An Aunt Jo, who was staying with the family, was the only one who encouraged Mary to even think of college. A fortuitous circumstance— a small bequest by her Aunt Jo—enabled her to realize the dream of going to college. She graduated summa cum laude from the local black school, North Carolina College, and subsequently received an MA and a Ph.D from the University of North Carolina.

And there is the rather defiant memoir of Richard Rodriguez of Mexican heritage. Rodriguez proudly proclaims that "once upon a time, I was a 'socially disadvantaged' child . . . and that thirty years later I write this book as a middle-class American."[44] Rodriguez and his three brothers and sisters performed well at the Catholic parochial school in Sacramento, California. That was due to the nuns as well as to the Rodriguez children's desire for learning. "My earliest teachers, the nuns, made my success their ambition," he writes.[45] That success was all the more remarkable since Rodriguez knew but fifty "stray" words of English when he started school.

Rodriguez's family can be best described as working-class poor. His father had steady work but mostly in low-paying occupations such as warehouse, cannery, factory, and janitorial jobs. Finally, when the children were grown, he became a dental technician. Rodriguez's mother was a housewife. She raised the children and provided a strong support for their desire for education. But that education helped place Rodriguez in a world far removed from that of his parents. He muses that this also was motivation for him, that he sought to escape the world of his fathers. "A primary reason for my success in the classroom," he confesses, "was that I couldn't forget that schooling was changing me and separating me from the life I enjoyed before becoming a student."[46]

The end result was a Ph.D. in English from Berkeley after an undergraduate career on scholarship at Stanford. Despising ethnic politics, Rodriguez spurned numerous academic offers motivated, he felt, more out of considerations for affirmative action—which he abhorred—than for his ability. Instead, he became a writer and a "brown Uncle Tom," "notorious among certain leaders of America's Ethnic Left."[47]

These are only a few of those who "made it," but they represent countless others. They are mentioned because they have written memoirs of their childhood and schooling. They flesh out statistical studies and give a sense of reality to the fact that there are some poor children who manage to use the schools and achieve some measure of worldly success. They have one thing in common: School played a crucial role in their intellectual development and their image of themselves.

Notes

1. Colin Greer, *The Great School Legend* (New York: Basic Books, 1972), p. 157.
2. Ibid., p. 108.
3. Ibid.
4. Ibid.
5. Michael Katz, *Class, Bureaucracy and Schools* (New York: Praeger, 1972), p. xviii.
6. Ibid.
7. Diane Ravitch, *The Revisionists Revised* (New York: Basic Books, 1978), pp. 91–93.
8. Michael Katz, review of Diane Ravitch's *The Revisionists Revised, Harvard Educational Review* 49, no. 2 (May 1979), p. 256.
9. Ibid., p. 263.
10. Nathan Glazer, review of *The Economic Basis of Ethnic Solidarity* by Edna Bonacich and John Modell, *A Piece of the Pie* by

Stanley Lieberson, and *The Ethnic Myth* by Stephen Steinberg, in *The New Republic*, July 4 and 11, 1981, p. 29.

11. Stephen Steinberg, *The Ethnic Myth* (New York: Atheneum, 1981).

12. Stephen Steinberg, *The Academic Melting Pot* (New Brunswick, N.J.: Transaction Books, 1977).

13. As quoted in Irving Howe with Kenneth Libo, *World of Our Fathers* (New York: Simon & Schuster, 1976), p. 199.

14. Ibid., pp. 51–52.

15. Michael R. Olneck and Marvin Lazerson, "The School Achievement of Immigrant Children: 1900–1939," in *History, Education and Public Policy*, ed. Donald R. Warren (Berkeley, Calif.: McCutchan, 1978), p. 172.

16. Ibid., p. 176.

17. Diane Ravitch, *The Great School Wars* (New York: Basic Books, 1974), p. 178.

18. Olneck and Lazerson, "School Achievement of Immigrant Children," p. 215.

19. Ibid., p. 191.

20. Selma C. Berrol, "Education and Economic Mobility: The Jewish Experience in New York City, 1880–1920," *American Jewish Historical Quarterly* 65, no. 3 (March 1976), p. 262.

21. Thomas Kessner, "New Yorkers in Prosperity and Depression: A Preliminary Reconnaissance," in *Educating an Urban People: The New York Experience*, ed. Diane Ravitch and Ronald K. Goodenow (New York: Teachers College Press, 1981), p. 98.

22. Berrol, "Education and Economic Mobility," pp. 258–59.

23. Sherry Gorelick, *City College and the Jewish Poor* (New Brunswick, N.J.: Rutgers University Press, 1981), p. 123.

24. Ibid.

25. Selma Berrol, "The Open City: Jews, Jobs, and Schools in New York City 1880–1915," in *Educating an Urban People: The New York Experience*, ed. Diane Ravitch and Ronald K. Goodenow (New York: Teachers College Press, 1981), p. 106.

26. Ibid., p. 105.

27. Ibid., p. 102.

28. Ibid.

29. Kessner, "New Yorkers in Prosperity and Depression," p. 90.

30. Ibid., p. 97.

31. Gorelick, *City College and the Jewish Poor*, p. 125.

32. Alfred Kazin, *A Walker in the City* (New York: Harcourt, Brace, 1951), p. 13.

33. Ibid., pp. 38–39.

34. Ibid., p. 17.

35. Norman Podhoretz, *Making It* (New York: Random House, 1967), p. 1.

36. Ibid., p. 7.

37. Ibid., p. 9.

38. Ibid., p. 8.

39. Ibid., p. 10.

40. Peter Steinfels, *The Neoconservatives* (New York: Simon & Schuster, 1979), p. 129.

41. Dick Gregory with Robert Lipsyte, *Nigger* (New York: E. P. Dutton, 1964), p. 39.

42. Claude Brown, *Manchild in the Promised Land* (New York: Macmillan, 1965).

43. Mary E. Mebane, *Mary* (New York: Viking Press, 1901), p. 149.

44. Richard Rodriguez, *Hunger of Memory: The Education of Richard Rodriguez* (New York: Bantam Books, 1983), p. 3.

45. Ibid., p. 44.

46. Ibid., p. 45.

47. Ibid., p. 4.

3
RECENT EFFORTS TO EDUCATE AMERICA'S URBAN POOR

A new breed of educational researcher has emerged in the late 1970s to propose that schooling can indeed have impact on the lives of the poor. These researchers suggest that school personnel with certain characteristics can go far in influencing youngsters from deprived backgrounds. One of this group, Professor Ronald Edmonds, has termed their work the study of *effective schools*. Their research also reveals how inexact social studies are. It is one thing to measure scientific subjects experimentally, but is quite another to obtain accurate results when dealing with people; the variables multiply and often cannot be controlled.

The findings of these effective schools researchers do not necessarily contradict earlier research. The educational historians (the Revisionists, for example), never meant to suggest that schools could not be reformed and educational policy shaped to become effective for children of the poor. Their message was that for the most part, schooling kept the poor in their place.

The most substantial evidence that public schools can work, despite students' socioeconomic background, is Michael Rutter's study of London schools, *Fifteen Thousand Hours*. The study was so named because Rutter and his associates estimated that fifteen thousand hours was the length of time a student spends in schools, and they assumed that such a large chunk of one's life should have some effect. *Fifteen Thou-*

sand Hours is a longitudinal study of twelve London secondary schools; Rutter and his colleagues followed twenty-seven-
hundred pupils from the end of elementary school through
secondary school. The study was conducted from 1970 to 1974,
with three additional years to interpret the research.

The study concludes that schools can make a difference regardless of a pupil's socioeconomic background, for some
schools were observed to be more successful than others. This
evidence seems to contradict Coleman's and Jenck's findings
that family background is the chief determinant of academic
achievement.

But the Rutter study had different goals and different
methodological approaches that mark it off from the Coleman
and Jencks studies. For one thing, Rutter and his colleagues
sought to examine more than mere academic achievement;
they were also interested in behavior. They examined these
five outcomes: attendance, school behavior, success in the
General Examination (the culminating examination of
secondary school), delinquency outside the school, and pupils' employment one year after leaving school. The family
background of the students was mostly poor: 28 percent of
families had mothers with a psychiatric disorder and the same
percentage had fathers convicted of some offense; more than
half lived in overcrowded homes. One-fourth of the families
were immigrants (with the greatest number from the West In-
dies), but many were also from Asia and Africa.[1]

The most obvious difference between the Coleman and
Rutter studies is that the former examined his subjects at a
fixed point in time whereas the latter made observations over
a period of seven years. The methodology differs in other significant respects. Coleman focused on one educational outcome: academic achievement as measured by standardized
tests of verbal ability. According to Rutter, such a measure of
scholastic achievement "bore little relationship to anything
most schools would aim to teach."[2] Coleman chose his crite-
rion because American pupils have no national examinations.
Since Britain does, Rutter decided to employ the General
Certificate examination as the measure of academic achieve-

ment. Such examinations are a better method of evaluating what the schools are trying to achieve.

Coleman employed a cross-sectional study of large proportions representing a sample of 645,000 pupils. The emphasis was on the individual child whereas for Rutter, the focus was the school. The Rutter study includes schools that were a part of a cluster. Although one cannot make a generalization about all English schools from such a sample, the mere existence of successful schools is extremely important.

While employing such sophisticated quantitative techniques as multiple linear regression, the Rutter study was also qualitative. School climate was measured by participant observation. It is interesting to note that Rutter measured ingredients of a school such as facilities, resources, and personnel—that went beyond the variables considered by Coleman and Jencks. Coleman found those factors to have little bearing on academic achievement. Jencks drew the conclusion that they were difficult to measure. "We did not look in any detail at things like morale, teacher expectations, school traditions, and school 'climate,'" Jencks writes. "Policy makers cannot usually control them, social scientists cannot usually measure them, and no one can be sure whether they cause achievement or only result from it."[3]

Rutter's measures of school climate as recorded by participant observers included pupil behavior in classrooms such as lateness, fighting, drawing graffiti, forgetting pencils, and talking. Observers noted whether schools were custodial or more open in their operation; whether they permitted use of the telephone, whether students could obtain a cup of hot tea, or whether they could move freely within the school. They also studied teacher behavior: whether teachers were punctual, taught the full period, corrected homework regularly, and used praise and rewards. Those schools with optimal outcomes had an open atmosphere, rigorous academic programs, and dedicated teachers. Most important, teachers in these favorable schools had high expectations of student achievement and behavior as measured by interviews.

Rutter's major conclusion is that the difference in school

outcomes is dependent on the underlying ethos of the school, regardless of students' socioeconomic background. Successful schools have educationally sound strategies, high teacher expectations of student achievement and behavior, and provide a pleasant climate. "Even when the comparisons between schools were restricted to children who were quite similar in family background and personal characteristics prior to secondary transfer, marked school variations remained," Rutter concludes. "This meant that children were more likely to show good behavior and good scholastic attainments if they attended some schools than if they attended others."[4] Nevertheless, Rutter and his colleagues are careful to say that schools cannot completely compensate for family background and social inequalities.

Some criticism of the Rutter study has been made on methodological grounds. Peter Cuttace echoes the main criticism of the study: Rutter refuses to make his data available for reanalysis because of its "confidentiality." Rutter argues that a reanalysis by other scholars "would make identification of particular schools possible."[5] Cuttace was also disturbed by the nonrepresentative nature of the sample; there was "no wider population to which inference is warranted."[6] However, Rutter's main point was to show that effective schools *exist*, not that they are indicative of a certain percentage of the urban school population. Other criticisms center on minor errors contained in the regression estimates.

Rutter's study complements another study of school climate, conducted in the United States by Wilbur Brookover of Michigan State University and his colleagues. The Brookover study, however, is not as extensive as is Rutter's; it is also not longitudinal. Nonetheless, it examines many of the same factors that Rutter and his colleagues observed. Most important, Brookover, like Rutter, concludes that schools can make a difference.

The Brookover study, conducted in an urban area in the southeast part of Michigan, differs methodologically from previous research. It attempts to measure social-psychological factors of school climate besides socioeconomic background; it concentrates on elementary schools (from an assumption that the schools have their greatest influence in those grades); and it uses a stratified random sample of those schools in order to have more universal results. Also, like Rutter, Brookover focuses on schools and the variance among them rather than on individual students. Nonetheless, the Brookover study considers social composition of the schools as well as personnel items including class size, teacher qualifications, and daily attendance. These inputs are compared to the school social structure and social climate. What is measured in terms of outcomes is academic achievement, self-concepts, and self-reliance (the latter two considered extremely important in performance by Coleman).

The study includes a state sample of sixty-eight schools, a black sample of thirty schools (majority black population), and a white sample of sixty-one schools (at least 50 percent white student population). Since the state department of education administered a standard test of reading and math skills to all students in the fourth and seventh grades, there could be no fairer way comparing students.[7]

The school social structure was observed in terms of a number of key variables: parental involvement in the school, ability or heterogeneous grouping, open or closed classroom procedures, structuring of the school day, and staff satisfaction with school structure. School climate variables consisted mainly of expectations of the various members of the school community.

Using multiple regression analysis, the Brookover study found differences in achievement among both black and white schools. Most important, these academic differences could be attributed to the influence of the school and not socioeconomic background, important though that is. Brookover et al. concluded:

The fact that some low SES white and black schools do demonstrate a high level of academic achievement suggests that the socioeconomic and racial variables are not directly causal forces in the school social system. We, therefore, conclude that the school social climate and the instructional behaviors associated with it are more direct causal links in the production of achievement behavior in reading and mathematics.[8]

The Brookover study further investigates the performance of four of the schools studied: two successful schools (one white and one black, with low-income students) and two low achieving schools (one white and one black, with low income students). Participant observation was the technique employed. Characteristics studied were teacher expectations, time spent in instruction, use of reward and punishment as classroom reinforcement, grouping procedures, principals' roles, commitment to learning, and use of teaching games. Of great significance were teacher expectations: The Brookover study observes that many teachers "write-off" poor students.

Many people believe, and much research suggests that students from poor families cannot learn very much; that those who 'make it' are the exceptions, not the rule; and that family background (when race is not a factor) is the primary determinant of achievement. Fortunately for the students . . . (at the successful schools) . . . most of the teachers apparently have not read the research on the subject and have not been informed of poor students' predestined failure.[9]

A pattern emerges from the Rutter and Brookover studies. Schools that have some measure of success, despite students' socioeconomic background, have common features. The teachers possess high expectations of students, spending most of their time in instruction and rigorous work, and the principals exert strong educational leadership. Underlying these schools is an ethos, a tone, a climate conducive to learning.

Other studies, less substantial in nature, indicate differences in school effectiveness with low-income student population. Lezotte, Edmonds, and Ratner analyzed pupil performance in twenty elementary schools in the Detroit Model Cities Neighborhood. These schools were characterized as "inner-city" and serve a black and minority student population. An effective school was considered to be one in which students reached the city average in math and reading. The researchers randomly sampled twenty-five hundred students of the ten-thousand in the Model City schools. Pupils were examined on the basis of standardized tests (Stanford Achievement Test and the Iowa Test of Basic Skills).[10]

Eight of the twenty schools were considered effective in math and nine in reading. Examining the relationship of school and family background more closely, the researchers looked at two schools, Duffield and Bunche, where minority populations were, respectively, 97 and 99 percent, and the percentages of those with low economic status were 19 and 20 percent.[11] Students at Duffield were four months above the city average in reading, and those at Bunche were three months below. That was a clear indication of variation in school effectiveness. However, the size of the sample does not permit us to make firm or general conclusions.

Another study, perhaps the first of its kind, indicates the direction such research has been taking since Coleman. In 1971, Weber studied four effective inner-city schools (where students performed at the national norm in terms of reading achievement based on standardized tests). Weber found that these schools had strong leadership from the principal, high teacher expectations, and an orderly and pleasant atmosphere. These characteristics share much in common with those found in the Brookover and Rutter studies.[12]

In this same vein, a study by the New York State Office of Education Performance Review shows that two schools in New York City serving similar low income populations differed in reading achievement based on standardized tests. These differences were attributed to the school's influence. The effective school had a plan to deal with reading problems, smoother administration with an emphasis on instructional strategies, and teachers with higher expectations.[13]

A more recent report of success with poor children concerns the Martin Luther King, Jr., School in New Haven. This school worked with James Comer's Yale Child Study Center in an experiment. James Comer, associate dean of the Yale Medical School, reported that the staff at this elementary school was able to raise pupil performance from nineteen months below the national average in reading in 1969 to two months below the norm in 1979. The school was 99 percent black and mostly low income.[14] The King School sought to restore trust and respect and a common educational goal among faculty, students, and parents. This was accomplished through a strategy that emphasized a management unit including parents, teachers, and administrators. A parental participation program was also highly successful. The climate of the school improved so much that both staff and pupil attendance rose dramatically, and there was less disruptive pupil behavior. Comer concludes that the program at King "clearly shows that inner city children can learn at significantly higher levels than is common."[15]

These research efforts have emboldened reformers to generalize the implications of their findings. Edmonds felt that underprivileged student family backgrounds does not relieve a school of its obligation to teach the children of the poor. Comer concludes that it is "the obligation of each school and school system" to replicate his success at King elementary school.[16]

Experiments in Effective Schools

The work of Rutter, Brookover, and Edmonds spurred school administrators to seek effective schools. Beginning in the 1979–1980 school year, administrators in a score of cities initiated versions of effective schools in consultation with educators such as Edmonds. The first projects were in Milwaukee and New York City, with administrators in St. Louis, Chicago, Pontiac, Michigan and Norfolk, Virginia, following suit (the Norfolk project, begun in the fall of 1983, was the first systemwide application in all elementary schools of an effective schools project). The chief problem of school administrators was to operationalize the research findings. Nevertheless, after a few years, preliminary evaluations indicate modest gains in academic achievement that warrant optimism for success.

Those cities perceived to have shown noticeable success are Milwaukee, New York, St. Louis, and Chicago, with other cities still in the process of developing effective schools projects. In the Milwaukee project, school administrators tried to design a program that embodied the key research findings: strong leadership by the principal, high teacher expectations, and rigorous work. School personnel selected eighteen elementary and two middle schools serving a high percentage of poor and minority students with low standardized test scores.

The Milwaukee project, called RISE (for Rising to Scholastic Excellence) involved many meetings with principals and staff where high expectations and emphasis on how time on task could be increased were among the discussion topics. In addition, substantial administrative and instructional support was provided, including full-time assistant principals and full-time reading resource teachers for each school. Overseeing the RISE project was a coordinating board composed of two principals, two curriculum specialists, and the project director.

What were the outcomes of RISE? A study by professors Eugene E. Eubanks and Daniel U. Levine suggests that RISE had a good start. After two years, RISE students in all but three or four schools had made noteworthy progress. In the lower reading categories, the percentage of third graders decreased from 36 in 1981 to 32 in 1982.[17] This compared with a one point decrease in all of Milwaukee public schools. This reduction in RISE students in the lowest performance category was true also in fifth- and seventh-grade reading and fifth-grade mathematics.[18] What must be remembered, however, is that in the RISE schools 40 percent of third, fourth, and fifth graders still scored in the lowest categories.[19]

In Chicago, as in Milwaukee, the school administration selected the schools to participate in an effective schools strategy. Forty-five schools, including thirty-six elementary, were chosen from those that ranked lowest in reading and math scores. Most of these schools were black or Hispanic, and 69 percent served poor families.[20]

In addition to application of the research findings of Rutter, Edmonds, and Brookover, a strong component involving parental and community support was provided in the Chicago Effective Schools Project. For example, parents must pick up their children's report cards at the school—thus guaranteeing contact between low-income families and the schools. Also, principals must allocate a minimum of 30 percent of their time to instructional leadership.

The Chicago Effective Schools Project also recorded academic achievement. In 1981–1982, the first year of ESP's im-

plementation, eight-year-olds gained seven months in reading compared with the previous year's five month gain. Also,
eleven-year-olds gained nine months in reading compared with
a previous seven months, and thirteen-year-olds gained eleven
months compared to a previous seven months.[21]

In St. Louis, four schools with a total enrollment of nineteen hundred were chosen to participate in Project SHAL (the
initials of the first word of each participating school). Almost
all students were black and from poor areas in north St. Louis.
Here, too, students improved by an average four percentile
points with the largest gains in reading comprehension.[22]

Three effective schools projects were begun in New York
City. The School Improvement Project entailed sixteen schools
from poor areas. In the Local School Development Project,
there were thirty-eight schools from low income neighborhoods. And the Comprehensive Planning Project worked with
five elementary and junior high schools. The first two projects had a high degree of parental involvement as compared
with none in Milwaukee. In the School Improvement Project, the schools were selected by the staff and parents; and
the School Improvement Committees that supervised the
project consisted of teachers, parents, and other constituen-
cies. In the Local School Development Project, parents along
with teachers were instrumental in planning and administration.

The New York City experience with effective schools strategies "also provided grounds for optimism."[23] In the School
Improvement Project, there was an average increase of sixteen percentage points between 1979 and 1982 of students
reading on grade level. The average citywide gain, in contrast, was only four points. In the Local School Developmen-
tal Project, the percentage of schools in which 40 percent or
more were reading on grade level increased from 42 to 67 between 1980 and 1982.[24]

Professors Eubanks and Levine found that some problems
existed in these effective schools projects. It was necessary to
devote a large share of resources to them, including considerable amounts of staff development time to help teachers
become more effective and substantial commitments of ad-

ministrative and instructional support and monitoring. Moreover, many questions remain, such as whether schools participating in the effective schools strategy should be selected on a voluntary or mandatory basis. Nevertheless, the researchers were optimistic. They concluded that "our first look at effective school approaches in Chicago, Milwaukee, New York and St. Louis indicates that many or most inner city elementary schools can become more effective instructionally."[25]

There are other signs of various schools being effective. One report, commissioned by *Phi Delta Kappan*, the educator's magazine, sought to identify "exceptional" elementary urban schools serving the poor.[26] The resulting study, *Why Do Some Urban Schools Succeed?* is divided into two parts: The first section includes eight case studies of "exceptional" schools and the second section reviews research studies dealing with exceptional schools and other case studies. Probably because the researchers were from a midwestern university, the eight case studies of exceptional schools were located in the Midwest (Indianapolis, Gary, West Terre Haute, and Fort Wayne, Indiana; Decatur and Chicago, Illinois; Cincinnati, Ohio; and Louisville, Kentucky).

Typical of the case studies is the Mary W. French Elementary School in Decatur, Illinois, where 41.9 percent of the student population was black and 26 percent received free lunch. By 1979, students were reading on grade level. Parents found that the most critical element in the school climate was the dedication of the teachers "who care . . . who have a sincere interest . . . who are concerned about their children."[27] Also, teachers and principals "believe the student can and will learn."[28] In addition, the leadership of the principal was cited as being extremely supportive of staff and seeking parent involvement.

An overview of the eight "exceptional" schools sought to identify common characteristics that made for a successful school. These include, first and foremost, strong leadership from the principal. The *Phi Delta Kappan* study asserts: "Without exception, each case study was clear and specific; the building principal does make a difference."[29] In addition, six other factors are cited for personnel: participatory decision-making; decentralized staff selection (staff was hand-picked); empathy of principal toward teachers and students; high expectations of children by principal and teachers; role expectations by the public of high performance by principal and teachers: and firm discipline policy in the schools. Besides personnel policy, factors for success include minimum competency goals for instructional programs and parental involvement in the schools. Regarding the latter, the study concludes, "Students whose parents have a positive interest in the school and who support the school will tend to achieve better."[30] However, the amount and kind of parental involvement is not specified but merely assumed as being a supportive function.

The second part of the *Phi Delta Kappan* study is a search through the literature of successful urban elementary schools, divided into three components: 1. an analysis of case studies; 2. a review of the research literature; and 3. interviews with "experts" from the federal government, "change agents," and social scientists. (The interviews can be dismissed as speculation and opinion.)

The analysis investigated 253 case studies, of which 59 were deemed applicable. Over half of the studies were conducted between 1971 and 1974. Most of the cases aimed at improving the school through direct intervention strategies, that is, programs that would not have otherwise been available on a regular basis. The findings of these case studies showed that leadership in the school was identified as being important in school success in one-third of the studies. Also deemed significant was parental involvement.

The research literature identified 515 reports of which 40 were applicable. One-third of the studies reported directly on the importance of the role of the principal. "Elementary school principals," the study concludes, "and other program leaders are influential in determining success in urban elementary schools and programs."[31] This also holds true for parental involvement and curricular goals that are clearly stated.

The conclusions of this second part of the *Phi Delta Kappan* study list twelve factors explaining the success of urban elementary schools. Among these factors are the leadership of the principal—deemed "crucial"—parental involvement, and "clearly stated curricular goals and objectives." These factors correspond to the findings of Rutter and Brookover.

Robert Benjamin, an educational journalist on the *Baltimore Sun*, conducted a "journey" through some urban effective schools. In his book *Making Schools Work*, Benjamin describes his visits to a "rare set of elementary schools in which the children of the urban poor are learning."[32] These schools Benjamin perceived to be "mavericks or outlaws," estimating that "there are perhaps only a couple of dozen in the whole country [and] . . . many large urban school systems cannot boast a single example."[33] Nonetheless, Benjamin believes that these "mavericks" serve as educational models for other schools. "There is little reason to believe their lessons could not apply to middle-class schools . . . few schools could not stand improvement."[34]

Benjamin limited his "journey" to elementary schools because of the importance of early education. He also assumed that problems at junior and senior high schools could be "traced back to the failure at the elementary level"—an assumption that might not be warranted due to the growing influence of the poverty culture as youths get older.[35] The poverty determination was arrived at by examining schools that had at least 60 percent of their students on free lunch and where at least half of the sixth graders had a history reading below their grade level.

Benjamin was a participant observer in the classroom, looking for the recipe for success along the main guidelines of effective schools research. That is, he sought to identify strong leadership from the principal, high teacher expectations, and rigorous academic work as the main influences for effective schooling. His report fleshes out the cold statistics and analyses of the effective schools movement.

Benjamin found one effective school to be the Beasley Academic Center on Chicago's South Side. This school exhibited academic competition among the children of the poor and featured a back-to-basics curriculum. Perhaps its success can be attributed in part to the district superintendent, who did not "buy" the "self-fulfilling prophecy" that "these kids can't learn."[36] The head of District 13 was a black grandmother who herself had been poor ("We were very poor") and had attended a ghetto school that was 100 percent black.[37] She went to college through a church-sponsored scholarship (with time out for a stint in the Women's Army Corps during World War II when the scholarship money ran out) and finished her schooling under the GI Bill. Her experience as part of the black poor convinced her that the poor could learn. She set out to prove this as district superintendent, concentrating on Beasley Academic Center. And Beasley's eighth graders achieved the highest reading scores in Chicago.

Benjamin found another effective school in New York's South Bronx—an area of such poverty as to claim the attention of President Carter. Here the pupils were Hispanic, yet read above their grade level. But the educational approach was a "smorgasbord." Everything was tried.

However, Benjamin's journey was not wholly successful. He revisited a school that Brookover had cited as effective when his team visited it. In the ensuing years, Edison School in Madison Heights, Michigan, had undergone profound and significant change. Benjamin describes what he discovered: "By the fall of 1979, something had happened to this elementary school. Edison still had the same principal; its teacher turnover had been low; its students came from the same kinds of background. But almost every one of the positive attributes identified by the university researchers was no longer to be found."[38]

What had happened was a shift in educational philosophy from stress upon academics to emphasis on the "affective domain." The principal was responsible for this switch. As a result, there were no schoolwide academic objectives; teachers, unmonitored, did what they wanted to do; and the climate was acrimonious. This lack of instructional leadership was reflected in the scores of the students.

In an interesting project, Professor Daniel U. Levine and Joyce Stark sought to verify the development of various experiments in the schools. Levine, it must be remembered, had conducted respected studies correlating low achievement with low income school population (see chapter 1). With a grant from the National Institute of Education, Levine and Stark investigated the effect of school resources on schools in New York City, Los Angeles, and Chicago. They looked at twenty-one elementary schools in District 19 in Brooklyn that were involved in Mastery Learning. Students in these schools had improved their reading abilities with the percentage on grade level increasing from 30 in 1979 to 41 in 1981, and the percentage who were two or more years below grade level declining from 20 in 1979 to 13 in 1981.[39] Moreover, students in the Chicago schools Levine investigated were a half year above grade level, and in Los Angeles there was an increase of those on grade level from thirty-five in 1979 to fifty-six in 1981.[40]

Levine and Stark's study in New York, for example, notes the strong support from the superintendent and participation and support from the teachers' union. The most salient features were attempts at parental involvement in students' learning and improving the quality of homework. Moreover, supervision had become more "outcome-based," and "outstanding administration leadership was observed both at the building and district level."[41] This resulted in an administrative staff that was "both *supportive* of teachers and skilled in providing a *structured institutional pattern* in which teachers could function effectively."[42] Levine and Stark conclude that those projects represented a "means to bring about *incremental school improvements* at a large number of inner city schools."[43]

Nevertheless, Levine and Stark profess a difficulty in programming for effective schools. The studies of effective scholars, Levine writes, "have not quite reached the state of providing much specific guidance for improving achievement in other schools."[44] Although "outstanding leadership" is generally admitted as a variable influencing achievement, they feel that "it is still unclear how organizational processes and arrangements to effectively focus instruction can be implemented on a widespread basis in big city schools."[45]

Head Start Success

Some indication that the children of the poor can be helped through schooling is shown through programs that have worked with both ends of the spectrum: preschoolers and a young adult population. The Head Start program and a program for dropouts in the army give hope that the poor can take advantage of schooling.

Perhaps the best known educational program that has worked with poor youngsters is Head Start. Begun in 1965, the Head Start program was designed to educate the children of the poor in preschool. (Middle-class parents had long been aware of the benefits of nursery or preschool experience.) In 1964, Benjamin Bloom presented hard evidence in *Stability and Change in Human Characteristics* that a child's early years are crucial in learning.[46] According to Bloom, children develop half of their intelligence by age four and 80 percent by age eight. Consequently, the sooner that poor youngsters can be exposed to the classroom, the greater the chance they can be redeemed from a life of poverty. How better to break the "poverty cycle" than by giving them a "head start" in the educational race and, eventually, a passport into a meritocratic society?

How Head Start fared was of great importance in the effort of educators to affect teaching the poor. In 1969, "The Impact of Head Start," a study conducted by Westinghouse Learning Corporation and Ohio University, branded the four-year-old program "experimental" and "extremely weak."[47] The investigators for this report on 104 Head Start centers found that the Head Start pupils in public schools were not any more proficient in language development, learning readiness, academic achievement, positive self-concept, desire for achievement, or attitudes toward school, home, peers, and society than those children not exposed to the Head Start experience. Most important, the dramatic increase of IQ among Head Start children evaporated in later years in public school. Yet, somewhat paradoxically, some black children in the cities and the Southeast benefited. These children made small advances that "were statistically significant and indicated that the program evidently had some limited effect on one of the most deprived groups in our society."[48]

A more thorough and methodologically sound analysis of longitudinal studies conducted by more than a dozen researchers came to an opposite conclusion. In *Lasting Effects After Preschool*, supervised by professors Irving Lazar and Richard B. Darlington, the original studies were followed up through interviews with children and parents, analysis of achievement test scores, and consideration of children's standing in school. The children were nine to nineteen years of age. All the programs were initiated and completed prior to 1969, with the students followed through 1976–1977.

Lazar and Darlington are more optimistic about the impact of Head Start. Surveying some three-thousand low-income children who were either in Head Start or control groups, their study found some positive academic and behavioral outcomes. Head Start children, for example, were least likely to be left back in school, and the IQ gains persisted for a full three years. Fourth graders who had a Head Start experience did significantly better on mathematics achievement tests, and a "suggestive" trend was indicated on fourth-grade reading tests. In three projects, the Head Starters maintained their IQ superiority. Moreover, Head Starters had better self-esteem, and their mothers had higher vocational aspirations than the children had for themselves. Lazar and Darlington conclude that "preschool intervention programs had significant long-term effects on school performance."[49] They also assert that "all lower-income children can benefit from preschool experience."[50] But the need is that "children must also be motivated to continue to learn and achieve in school. They must believe that school is important and possess enough self-confidence to exert the necessary effort."[51]

The armed forces have obtained some startling results. Sociologist Roger Little studied the armed forces' celebrated Project 100,000, which was conceived in 1966 because of a manpower shortage in the Vietnam War. It entailed admitting 100,000 recruits with limited educational background or low educational achievement, known in military terms as Category IV.[52] This project was developed in terms of both military needs and as an experiment in basic education.

Forty percent of the trainees were nonwhite. A year later, approximately 49,000 men had been processed under the new standards. These standards were twofold: high school graduates were admitted without further testing, and non-high school graduates with low scores on the Armed Forces Quotient Test were required to score ninety or higher on one or more aptitude tests. Approximately 32 percent of these recruits had failed one grade of school, and 17 percent had failed two grades. Over 29 percent were unemployed, and an additional 27 percent were earning poverty wages.[53]

The success of Project 100,000 was overwhelming. In basic training, 96 percent graduated, with a dropout rate of 3 percent, only one percentage point above the military average. In advanced training, 74 percent of students in communications, intelligence, and medical fields graduated, as did 89 percent in administration and clerical fields, 78 percent in electrical and mechanical equipment fields, 88 percent in crafts, and 55 percent in electronic equipment repair. The armed forces had converted uneducables" into productive citizens.[54]

According to Professor Little, the structured military community imbued the trainees with new and powerful identities: those of soldiers. Success of the project could be attributed, in large measure, to this "opportunity for developing self-esteem and a feeling of group participation."[55] Moreover, the attitudes of the military teachers were crucial. The armed forces teachers treated the Project 100,000 recruits as they would any others. Neither were these teachers aware of any special status to the group. In short, the new recruits were expected to learn, and they did.

Sociologist Little speculates on other reasons for the success of Project 100,000 recruits. He cites the plenitude of food in the army compared with its lack in slum life; the esteem derived from the uniform; the organization of military life compared with the disorganization of ghetto life; the integrated nature of the armed forces; the protection of the recruit's medical needs, welfare, and insurance; and the fairness of the military system. In terms of the implications for public policy, Little feels that the military provides a "second chance" to many youngsters. He estimates that approximately 20 percent of young men of lower-class background who have failed in public schools could have this "second chance." However, he cautions that the military's educational success cannot be replicated in the present structure of public education. Perhaps what could be done would be to create some form of "comprehensive institutional setting."

Private and Parochial Schools

What of private schools? Little research has been conducted on the arcane world of private schools. Now that private schools are eager to obtain either direct federal help or aid in the form of tuition tax credits, a few studies have appeared concerning their education of the children of the poor. Admittedly, few poor students attend private schools—for the obvious reason that tuition is most often beyond their means. But certain school plants, like the Catholic parochial schools, remain in the cities long after their clienteles have made the trek to the suburbs. As a result, these schools face the challenge of providing schooling to a new minority poor.

Private schools that serve low income students are reporting scattered success in raising the educational levels of these students. *Public and Private High Schools*, an interesting recent study by James Coleman et al., attests to the power of schools in influencing academic achievement. This study is the first of a five part longitudinal study of high school sophomores and seniors. Commissioned by the National Center for Educational Statistics, it compares private, parochial, and public schools with a total of 58,728 sophomores and seniors; 1,016 high schools in the sample. It is a two staged stratified probability sample not without its limitations. The sample is restricted since some students declined to participate.

The new Coleman study contradicts his previous report, *Equality of Educational Opportunity*. *Public and Private High Schools* concludes that private and parochial schools "produce better cognitive outcomes than the public schools."[56] Most important, this influence holds true even when family background is taken into consideration.

When family background factors that predict achievement are controlled, students in both Catholic and other private schools are shown to achieve at a higher level than students in public schools. The difference at the sophomore level, which was greater for the Catholic schools than for other private schools, ranged from about a fifth of the sophomore-senior gain to about two-thirds the size of that gain (i.e., from a little less than half a year's difference to something more than one year's difference).[57]

The measures used for educational achievement among sophomores and seniors were standardized tests in reading, vocabulary, and math. The result was that "achievement was somewhat higher in both the sophomore and senior years in Catholic schools and in other private schools than it is in public schools."[58] The study is careful to note that this success could be attributed to factors—such as motivation—associated with self-selection in entering a private or parochial school. Most important, although family background does not account for the influence of these schools, it is not to be interpreted necessarily that the poor succeed in school. Catholic schools account for less than 6 percent of students with incomes below $12,000, whereas private schools account for 3 percent of these students. And both kinds of schools account for less than 5 percent of racial or ethnic minorities.

The study attempted to measure a number of variables. Coleman and his colleagues were interested in whether private schools are better educationally (yes); whether their students have more self-esteem (little evidence); whether these schools are safer and more ordered (yes); whether they are better in creating interest in learning (no evidence); whether they are better in encouraging interest in higher education (no strong evidence); whether they "cream" higher income students (yes); whether they are divisive religiously (yes); whether they are divisive racially (yes); whether they fail to provide the educational range of public schools (yes); and other behavioral measures.

The study strongly recommends a tuition tax credit or school voucher system, partly as a means to increase black and lower income student representation in private schools. This advocacy research was severely criticized by educators who wanted "pure research" and not policy studies. Others, speaking in behalf of public schools, were even more caustic. Albert Shanker, president of the American Federation of Teachers, wrote:

> It's not hard to see how Coleman achieved his results. It's hard to understand why he wasted his time, or why anybody would pay attention to the obvious. Just as there is a much higher percentage of sick people in hospitals (because that's what the hospitals are for), there's a much higher percentage of good students in private schools, because if you admit good students, reject poor risks, and expel those who don't meet standards, you're bound to end up with better students than schools which accept everyone.[59]

Only 10 percent of the student body in elementary and secondary schools attends private schools. Of these, nearly 90 percent attend Catholic parochial schools. However, there has been scant literature on how effective Catholic schools have been, especially with the urban poor. Evidence now accumulating shows that Catholic schools have indeed been *effective* in educating an urban poor.

Perhaps the most systematic analysis was conducted by the Rev. Andrew Greeley as part of the Coleman study of high school students just mentioned. Father Greeley, a long-term advocate of Catholic education, again finds evidence to support his thesis that Catholic schools are doing a good job, even with educating those disadvantaged students intent on upward mobility. Greeley's part of the Coleman study—isolating Catholic school students—employed the same sample of eleven hundred high schools with thirty-thousand sophomores and twenty-eight thousand seniors. Fifteen percent of these students in Catholic schools were black and Hispanic (6 percent and 9 percent respectively).[60] Again, approximately 6 percent of Catholic school students were poor—a very small number.

Especially interesting in the Greeley study is that he and his colleagues factored in student input as a crucial variable. That is, family background and student motivation—what the child brings to the school, the traditional Coleman-Jencks view of student achievement—were considered as the chief variables for effectiveness. Nevertheless, his sophisticated statistical study employing multiple-regression techniques comes to an opposite conclusion. "There are some aspects of the Catholic educational environment that cannot be accounted for merely in terms of student background characteristics," says Greeley.[61] There is a "tilt in the direction of a real school effect," he goes on, "and indeed an instructional effect."[62] In short, school power.

Moreover, input variables do not account for Catholic schools having a positive influence on students who are poor and minority. Greeley found that "correlations between social class and achievement are much *lower* among Catholic school students"[63] (emphasis added). In fact, the greatest success was among minority students whose fathers did not attend college. Greeley posits the tantalizing question "Is it just possible that there might be something going on in the classrooms of Catholic schools from which other educational institutions in this country might learn?"[64]

What one does learn in Greeley's report is that Catholic high schools tend to be more demanding than ordinary public schools. Catholic students report rigorous work more often than public-school students in the Coleman survey. They claim that they participate more in laboratory work and field trips, have more strenuous papers, and that their teachers require more homework. It will be remembered that strenuous classroom work was an important factor in effective public schools.

However, the Greeley study is limited in its applicability. Poor minority families who send their children to Catholic high schools encounter annual tuition averaging $1,000—which they must meet through some means, perhaps through full or partial scholarships. That assumes a high degree of parental participation and motivation. Moreover, the students, as Greeley notes, are the most academically motivated to begin with. Usually it is the more affluent minority members who send their children to Catholic schools. And most important, they are high school students—they have made it academically beyond elementary and junior high school, no small feat in itself. Nevertheless, Greeley says that Catholic schools have an effect despite these factors.

Yet the Catholic school system has also undertaken a large

task in the cities to educate the poor in elementary schools. A report by the Rev. Timothy O'Brien surveys a random selection of inner-city Catholic schools in eight cities: Los Angeles, New Orleans, Chicago, Milwaukee, Detroit, New York, Newark, and Washington, D.C. The enrollment totaled over 15,000 students, 70 percent of whom were classified as minority. In addition, some 4,000 elementary school parents, 339 teachers, and 55 principals responded to an attitudinal survey.

One-third of the families in these Catholic urban schools were Protestant. Of the black families, 53 percent were Protestant and 44 percent Catholic. Understandably, 98 percent of the Hispanic families were Catholic and 92 percent of the white families. Most important, 15 percent of the families reported incomes under $5,000, and 35 percent reported incomes under $10,000. Thus, 50 percent could be considered low income families. It is noteworthy that 72 percent of the families reported incomes of less than $15,000, and that 35 percent were one-parent families with only the mother present.[65]

This study reports dramatic instances of academic achievement, with St. Leo's in Milwaukee a case in point. St. Leo's, reopened in 1977, had a 98 percent black enrollment, with 85 percent qualifying for free meals under the federal breakfast and hot-lunch program. The Iowa Test of Basic Skills was administered to transfer students at the beginning and end of the school year. Fourth graders were two years behind grade level at the outset, but by the end of the year were three months behind in reading and four months behind in math. Although more than two years behind, sixth graders finished the year only nine months under grade level. Seventh graders lagged two and a half years scholastically, yet within ten months were just one year below expected achievement levels.[66]

Another analysis of Catholic schools in the inner city shows marked success. In Manhattan, pupils in 79 percent of forty-seven inner-city Catholic grade schools were from minority groups, with most being low income. One school in the Bronx—Our Lady of Victory—operated jointly with the Congress of Racial Equality, showed that the low income students were only one year behind in national norms whereas children from nearby public schools were three years behind.[67] Catholic school students in the inner city generally score higher on standardized tests than do pupils from public schools in the same neighborhood.

Other Advances

The plethora of federal programs initiated by the Johnson administration seems to have had some effect. The National Assessment of Educational Progress measured nine-year-olds, comparing results of reading tests administered in 1970–1971, 1974–1975, and 1979–1980. One remarkable result was that nine-year-old black students raised their average scores by 9.9 percent. Educational and political figures attributed this gain to the impact of Title I of the Elementary and Secondary School Act.[68] This "reading recovery" was replicated in some of the most disadvantaged areas of New York City, where pupils recorded an improvement in reading scores for the second year in a row in 1980, and where, for the first time, a majority were at or above grade levels. In depressed areas like East Harlem, the scores rose 9 percent, placing 44 percent of pupils at grade level. In Ocean Hill-Brownsville, P.S. 155 went up 10 percent in pupil reading scores to 38.4 percent at grade level; that was duplicated at P.S. 134 in the Bronx, where students raised their scores 9.4 percent to reach a total of 32.7 percent of students at grade level.[69]

City University provides a dramatic example of educating an urban poor. An indication that a significant number of poor students attend college is shown by a breakdown of family income of students attending City University in New York City. It must be remembered that city colleges were tuition free in New York until 1976, the year of the financial crisis in New York City government. Despite the imposition of tuition, a large number of City University students are still either poor or near poor. Over 30 percent of students at senior colleges had a family income under $8,000 in 1979—a figure considered more realistically as a poverty line by many observers; nearly 47 percent of students at these colleges had family incomes under $11,000—near poor; and over 62 percent had incomes under $16,000 a year. The community colleges reported similar statistics in 1979. Over 40 percent of students at community colleges had family incomes under $8,000, over 60 percent under $11,000, and over 73 percent under $16,000. This is hardly economic security. For black students, the figures are in line with the general statistics. Over 40 percent of black students in the senior colleges and over 60 percent in community colleges came from families with a total income under $8,000—a modern index of poverty in large cities.[70] These figures show that a substantial number of poor students and near poor (City University has an enrollment close to 180,000) are in colleges and universities.

The national figures for first-time college students support that thesis. Of nearly 2 million students in 1978 (the last year for which such figures were available), 16 percent were from families who made less than $10,000, and 25 percent were from families who made less than $12,000.[71]

The first survey of City University *graduates* indicated that a large number were poor and minority. Forty-seven percent of community college graduates and 31 percent of students in four-year colleges in the class of 1979 were from minority groups.[72] That year, CUNY accounted for over half of the degrees from four-year colleges in New York City, where there are many private colleges; moreover, the proportion of minority students at CUNY is approximately three times the proportion that graduates from colleges nationally.[73]

A significant number of the CUNY graduates—36 percent —entered the university with poor academic preparation (that is, with high school averages below 80 percent).[74] Two-thirds of the graduates came from homes where neither parent had attended college, and one-fifth were from homes where the highest level their parents attained was elementary school. Part of their success was due to remediation efforts whereby a solid majority of both community college and four-year college graduates took remedial courses while at the university. Over 80 percent of the graduates, moreover, want to continue their education and pursue an additional degree.[75] The social mobility of the graduates was noticeable in their employment. At the date of the survey, three-fourths were employed full-time with an average annual income above $14,000.[76]

As we have observed, the poor have achieved at respectable levels educationally. They have done this in preschool (Head Start), in certain effective schools, and in private and parochial schools. This attests to the power of education—under the right conditions—despite the socioeconomic background of students. And it dispatches the myth that the poor are, by and large, uneducable.

Notes

1. Michael Rutter et al., *Fifteen Thousand Hours* (Cambridge, Mass.: Harvard University Press, 1979), pp. 33–34.

2. Ibid., p. 3.

3. Christopher Jencks et al., *Inequality* (New York: Basic Books, 1972), pp. 95–96.

4. Rutter, *Fifteen Thousand Hours*, p. 178.

5. Peter Cuttace, "Reflections on the Rutter Ethos," *Urban Education* 16, no. 4 (January 1982), p. 483.

6. Ibid., p. 486.

7. Wilbur Brookover et al., *School Social Systems and Student Achievement* (New York: Praeger, 1979), pp. 9–10.

8. Ibid., p. 142.

9. Ibid., p. 86.

10. Ronald Edmonds, "Some Schools Work and More Can," *Social Policy* (March-April 1979), pp. 30–31.

11. Ibid.

12. George Weber, *Inner-City Children Can Be Taught to Read: Four Successful Schools* (Washington, D.C.: Council for Basic Education, 1971).

13. Edmonds, "Some Schools Work and More Can," p. 28.

14. James Comer, "On Inner-City Education," *New York Times*, September 23, 1980, p. A23.

15. Ibid.

16. Ibid.

17. Eugene E. Eubanks and Daniel U. Levine, *A First Look at Effective School Projects at Inner City Elementary Schools* (Kansas City, Mo., 1983), p. 8.

18. Ibid.

19. Ibid., p. 9.

20. Ibid., p. 10.

21. Ibid., p. 15.

22. Ibid., p. 22.

23. Ibid., p. 28.

24. Ibid., p. 33.

25. Ibid., p. 39.

26. Phi Delta Kappa, *Why Do Some Urban Schools Succeed?* (Bloomington, Ind.: Phi Delta Kappa, 1980).

27. Ibid., p. 80.

28. Ibid., p. 81.

29. Ibid., p. 132.

30. Ibid., p. 139.

31. Ibid., p. 176.

32. Robert Benjamin, *Making Schools Work* (New York: Continuum, 1981), p. 1.

33. Ibid., p. 102.

34. Ibid., p. 9.

35. Ibid., p. 8.

36. Ibid., p. 18.

37. Ibid., p. 17.

38. Ibid., p. 126.

39. Daniel U. Levine and Joyce Stark, *Instructional and Organizational Arrangements for Improving Achievement at Inner City Elementary Schools* (Kansas City, Mo., 1982), p. 3.

40. Ibid.

41. Ibid., p. 12.

42. Ibid.

43. Ibid., p. 15.

44. Ibid., p. 1.

45. Ibid.

46. Benjamin Bloom, *Stability and Change in Human Characteristics* (New York: John Wiley and Sons, 1964).

47. Maurice R. Berube, "Head Start to Nowhere," *Commonweal* (May 30, 1969), p. 311.

48. Ibid., p. 312.

49. Irving Lazar and Richard B. Darlington, *Lasting Effects After Preschool* (Ithaca, N.Y.: Cornell University, October 1978), p. 2.

50. Ibid., p. 134.

51. Ibid., p. 83.

52. Roger Little, "Basic Education of Youth Socialization in the

Armed Forces," *American Journal of Orthopsychiatry* 38, no. 5 (October 1968), p. 871.

53. Ibid.

54. Ibid., pp. 871–72.

55. Ibid.

56. James Coleman et al., *Public and Private High Schools* (Chicago: ERIC Document Reproduction Service, ED 197–403, March 1981), p. 18.

57. Ibid.

58. Ibid., p. 286.

59. Albert Shanker, "Which Coleman Report Do We Believe?" *New York Times*, April 12, 1981, p. E9.

60. Andrew M. Greeley, *Catholic High Schools and Minority Students* (New Brunswick, N.J.: Transaction Books, 1982), p. 9.

61. Ibid., p. 57.

62. Ibid., p. 58.

63. Ibid., p. 74.

64. Ibid., p. 111.

65. Virgil C. Blum and Timothy O'Brien, *Inner City Private Elementary Education* (Milwaukee, Wis., 1980), pp. 1–3.

66. Ibid., pp. 5–6.

67. Robert Hoyt, "Learning a Lesson from the Catholic Schools," *New York*, September 12, 1977, pp. 49–50.

68. Gene I. Maeroff, "Reading Data Indicate Decline in Reasoning," *New York Times*, April 29, 1981, p. A20.

69. New York City Public Schools, *Pupil Reading Achievement* (New York: Board of Education, 1981).

70. City University of New York, *CUNY Data Book* (New York: City University of New York, 1981), pp. 114–17.

71. National Center for Education Statistics, *Digest of Education Statistics 1980* (Washington, D.C.: U.S. Government Printing Office, 1981), pp. 90–91.

72. Barry Kaufman et al., *Outcomes of Educational Opportunity: A Study of Graduates from the City University* (New York: City University Report, October 1981), p. v.

73. Ibid.

74. Ibid., p. vi.

75. Ibid., pp. vi-vii.

76. Ibid., p. ix.

4
A CRITIQUE OF THE EFFECTIVE SCHOOLS MOVEMENT

One must be cautious concerning the rush to effective schools. First, the task of operationalizing the research results is formidable considering the vagueness of many of the conditions associated with effective schools. Second, the need for further research to refine our knowledge about what makes for truly successful education for the urban poor is essential. And third, one must look at the other side of the equation—student motivation—and how it impinges on the learning process.

The new wave of research on effective schools needs careful evaluation. None of the studies established a direct causal link between the variables that are associated with effective schools and the success of those schools. These variables (which we shall examine more closely)—educational leadership from the principal, orderly school climate, high teacher expectations, and rigorous academic work—are to be found in effective schools. But it does not necessarily follow that they have caused that academic success. Indeed, Robert Benjamin's follow-up investigation of an effective school cited by Wilbur Brookover in his Michigan study showed dismal performance a few years after the Brookover study. Although there was a notable shift in educational priorities by the same principal, this example raises the question of whether one can expect effective schools to be effective over a long period.

Critics of effective schools research contend that perhaps it is "too soon to cheer." Stewart C. Purkey and Marshall S. Smith found that most of the effective schools research is far from conclusive.[1] (It may be recalled that Smith was a co-author with Christopher Jencks of *Inequality*, which claims that social class background is the greatest influence upon a child's learning abilities.) These critics maintain that the effective schools research is narrow because of its small samples, that inappropriate comparisons are made with bad schools rather than with average ones, and that "the generalizability of the research is limited."[2] But as has been pointed out in the case of the Rutter study, the aim of the effective schools researchers was to make a general statement that *some* schools exist that can adequately prepare students from low income backgrounds. Perhaps the most pertinent comment of these critics is that there is a dearth of longitudinal studies. Rutter's study is the only one of note, and the work of Brookover, Edmonds, and Comer does not qualify as such. Certainly more longitudinal studies are needed, since they have the benefit of greater reliability.

Still, the effective schoolers have satisfactorily established that successful schools, albeit few in number, do exist in low income urban areas. That proposition carries with it certain inevitable questions. Are these schools exceptions— mavericks—from which generalizations to most urban schools *cannot* be made? Or do these maverick effective schools suggest an educational pattern that can be replicated successfully for the great majority, or a substantial number, of urban schools that serve the poor? Many of the effective schoolers believe the latter to be the case.

Let us examine some of the prescriptions for change that the effective schoolers suggest. Professors Lawrence Lezotte and Wilbur Brookover seek to examine the "process of changing *low-achieving* schools into *high-achieving* schools."[3] In order to accomplish that objective, Lezotte and Brookover recommend changing "the school social system," the instructional climate of schools, and the classroom climate.

But are not these variables precisely those that least lend themselves to control by public policy, as Christopher Jencks charged? Lezotte and Brookover are sufficiently sophisticated to realize that resistance to educational change is to be expected. They believe that most school people "are truly concerned with the welfare of their students but they perceive threats to job security, have a vested interest in the status quo, and tend to revere the past."[4]

Nevertheless, what these researchers propose is a sort of greening of educational America. The first—and perhaps the only—step they strongly urge is a "widespread dissemination of information that low-income, minority students do achieve well in some schools."[5] Since the majority of school people believe otherwise (and have been buttressed in that belief by the research of Coleman and Jencks), such a greening of educational America is essential. Lezotte and Brookover strongly emphasize that "change must occur in the beliefs, attitudes and patterns that characterize the school social system."[6] One practical suggestion they offer is for teachers to observe one another in classrooms, as was successfully tried in an innovative teacher in-service project in California.

James Comer's success with an elementary school for the poor in New Haven emboldened him to offer his solution to educating low income minority students. His recipe for success differs slightly from that of his fellow effective schoolers in that it embodies a Theory Z management style, that is, highly participatory decision-making and meaningful parental involvement. Comer's program benefited from a lack of an authoritarian leader, and embodied a process model whereby "all levels of school personnel, directly or through representatives, participate in making decisions about school issues."[7] Unfortunately, much of the initiative was supplied by Comer's Yale Child Study Center—an "outside" catalyst to the schools. Moreover, American business, which is the first to adopt innovative management styles from which educational management normally follows, has yet to convert to the Japanese Theory Z management style of participatory decision-making.

More hopeful is the parent program that Comer installed in New Haven. Attempting to "bring the vitality of the community as it has existed naturally in the past into the school," Comer devised a program whereby "parents became involved in school policy and practice," and were therefore "sharing power."[8] For example, the personnel committee that hired new teachers was composed of two parents, two teachers, and the principal. Certainly parental participation is an educational goal that can muster a constituency for educational change.

Robert Benjamin, the educational journalist sympathetic to the effective schoolers, goes beyond the findings of these researchers to recommend two highly structured educational programs that have achieved a modicum of success with low-income children. These are Mastery Learning and DISTAR (Direct Instruction for Teaching and Remediation). Both programs are objective-oriented, structured with an emphasis on minimum competencies, and "force-feed" basics to the children of the poor. Mastery Learning was devised chiefly by Benjamin Bloom and DISTAR mainly by Siegfried Engleman. According to Benjamin, "DISTAR works . . . it was the only program that showed it could bring poor children up to the average achievement levels of their middle-class peers with some regularity."[9]

These are somewhat controversial programs. Critics of Mastery Learning and DISTAR cite their panacea approach as a flaw. They resent not only the mechanistic, joyless style of these programs but their refusal to consider different approaches. Different children, critics contend, flourish under different learning styles. Nonetheless, the prescriptions of such as Lezotte, Comer, Bloom, and Engelman help to reestablish a dialogue on school reform and are a healthy sign.

The effective schoolers confront many difficulties. In addition to the problems of translating vague research findings into public educational policy, they are a small band of academics in search of a constituency. The politics of education in this country in the past two decades suggests that the teacher organizations—the American Federation of Teachers and its larger and more powerful rival, the National Education Association—will resist change. The leadership of these organizations has been cool in the past to suggestions that teachers can do better than they are doing. This reaction is a self-defense mechanism to protect teachers from harsh criticism as well as to shield the policies of the teacher leadership.

Consider, for example, the case of Marva Collins, a black former public school teacher who launched her own private school for poor black youth in Chicago. She claimed a modicum of success, and television was quick to tell her story, on the immensely popular "60 Minutes" and in a TV drama watched by 19 million people. Critics later charged that her success story had little hard evidence to support it. Surely, in the absence of a controlled research study, the decision by the television networks to highlight her story was premature, to say the least, especially when there were other examples of effective schooling substantiated by hard data.

What is instructive, however, is the reaction of teacher leaders. Albert Shanker, president of the American Federation of Teachers, was highly delighted by Marva Collins's embarrassment. In his paid column in the Sunday *New York Times*, Shanker quickly labeled the Collins story a "fable" that had a bad effect on the "millions of teachers who strive to educate our youth."[10] He claimed there were "no miraculous answers to tough educational problems" and said teachers should not be "demoralized and undermined by media-created myths and fairy tales."[11] (It must be noted that the AFT has outdone the rival NEA in the last two decades in opposing every major attempt to reform the schools. At best, the AFT seeks to preserve the status quo; at worst, it has been educationally reactionary and, at times, racist in its actions.)

Most school reformers now believe that educational change must emerge from beyond the confines of the leadership of teacher groups. Such a coalition can draw on the best from business, public life, and parents *and* from teachers directly.

One method of reaching teachers is through schools of education. They too, however, are sadly in need of reform. Most have no programs in urban education, and some critics have charged that many professors of education are not even familiar with current research findings in education generally. That may be due partly to the newness of educational research. (Although educational research began at the turn of the century, most was of the survey variety, limited in scope and usefulness. Serious experimental as well as historical research in the field actually is a product of the 1960s.)

The pioneer work of the effective schoolers does need refinement. One needs to find out more, for example, about just what makes one principal in an urban school so successful in creating a learning climate along with teachers whereas another may not be so effective.

Let us examine the conditions for effective schools in terms of *Realpolitik*.

The Principal as Educational Leader

Very little research on the educational effectiveness of the principal has been available. It is only since the 1960s that systematic study of the role of the principal has been made.[12] One recent study by Arthur Blumberg and William Greenfield, *The Effective Principal*, reflects the difficulty of assessing principal effectiveness. This is a qualitative study of eight principals (three male and one female elementary school principals and two male and two female secondary school principals) selected on the basis of their reputations as dynamic individuals in the schools as perceived by teachers and administrators. The measure of their outstanding ability is shown by the fact that half left their jobs for more lucrative business opportunities by the time of the publication of the study.

After a review of the growing literature on principalship in recent years, the authors catalogued the principals by means of outstanding characteristics. For example, one black principal who sought change was described as the Catalyst. Another, who brokered relations between the superintendent and teachers, was labeled the Broker, and so on. These portraits did not lend themselves to quantitative methods but to qualitative interviews and "shadowing of the principals." The study did not correlate effectiveness with educational achievement of pupils, nor were all the schools in the inner city.

The study concludes that these individuals were mavericks— exceptions to the rule—and that the dichotomy between the art and the science of school administration favored, in these cases at least, the art. What is instructive for our purposes, however, is that the authors sought to provide a guide on management of the schools with little relation to educational leadership. They perceived that the role of the principal had evolved through the years into three distinct functions: as manager, supervisor, and broker to the school community.

We need in the future qualitative studies of effective school principals who have successful educational outcomes. Through means of case studies involving interviews and by following the principal throughout a school day to record educational behaviors, we might gather a glimmer of insight into what makes an educationally effective principal.

Nearly everyone in education concurs that the principal is the key educational person in the school. Future studies should concentrate on his or her educational leadership. Since these studies must be qualitative, their representativeness might be questioned. Nonetheless, such studies are needed if we are to be able to program educational policy for success.

One key drawback of the Blumberg-Greenfield study is that they never bothered to obtain each principal's philosophy of education. They were so intent on interviewing their case studies for management philosophy that they failed to obtain any personal views of learning.

Teacher Expectations

There is growing evidence that student achievement is influenced by teacher expectations. The tone and level of performance expected by teachers influence students' performance. The most dramatic study of teacher expectations was conducted by Robert Rosenthal and Lenore Jacobson and published in the late sixties as *Pygmalion in the Classroom*. That study, however, seemed to suffer from methodological faults and was never successfully replicated. However, Michael Rutter reviewed several self-fulfilling prophecy studies such as conducted by W. J. Seaver.[13] Whereas in the Rosenthal study, teachers were deliberately misled by falsified test scores, the cases studied by Rutter were "natural" processes. The Rosenthal-Jacobson study shows that few teachers believe studies that run counter to their teaching experience. I have found that most teachers feel that their own experience in the classroom gives them a realistic indication of student achievement levels.

A crucial factor to be considered is the degree of racism that may exist in urban classrooms. Although racism obviously exists in our society, it is difficult to ascertain the degree and variety of racial feeling that teachers and administrators may harbor. In the United States, there has been clear evidence of institutionalized racism. One need only consult Professor Stanley Lieberson's fine study A Piece of the Pie to learn of its prevalence.

However, there is some dispute over whether large-scale racial discrimination still exists. Conservatives and neoconservatives contend that racial discrimination is no longer a factor in American life. While laws now guarantee voting rights and prohibit employment discrimination, the evidence does not seem to support the contention that institutional racism has been eliminated in the United States. Blacks are overrepresented in the poverty polls. Since only the 1980s have slightly more than 9 percent of students in universities been black, corresponding closely to their 10 percent of the population.[14] Moreover, official government figures, which some critics maintain are too low, indicate that one-third of the black population lives in poverty.[15] As for attitudes of individual whites toward blacks, a 1982 survey of Ivy League graduates of the late fifties reveals racist attitudes. Only 37 percent of Princeton graduates, 46 percent of Yale graduates, and 54 percent of Harvard graduates believed that blacks are as intelligent as whites.[16] (These products of elite universities are now in leadership positions in American society.)

Nevertheless, teacher expectations may be controlled by policy more than one would think. A greening of educational America to the belief that low income students can achieve would be necessary. It should involve promulgation of research and experience—as has been done by the effective schoolers to a certain extent—and should be national in scope. On the other hand, school systems could have in-service courses on the research findings to reinforce the belief that many students who are poor can achieve at respectable levels. That is definitely in the realm of educational policy and would only require the initiative of bold school superintendents. It would do much to bridge the chasm between the two cultures, for middle-class teachers and poor students have not in our history worked well together.

Rigorous Work

This variable is perhaps the one most easy to control for educational policy makers. Through in-service education (as that sponsored by the RISE effective schools project in Milwaukee), teachers can grasp the essential concept of the need to spend most class time on educational projects—time on task. Indeed, the research shows that this is a crucial factor. In *A Place Called School*, John Goodlad points out that there is a strong relationship between time on task in the classroom and learning.

Moreover, many urban school districts, such as New York City, have begun to require homework from their pupils. Beginning in 1983 in New York City, the amount of homework time mandated by the school board varied with the grades and ages of the students. A system of checking on teachers so that they would implement the new policy was also devised. This policy marked a first step for New York City schools and was in recognition of the research by the effective schoolers.

Parent Participation

Parental involvement in schooling has always been regarded as essential to learning, and educators have long claimed to encourage it. However, definitions of parental involvement in the schools range from occasional bake sales at the PTA to a concept of community controlled urban schools where elected parents form school boards with power over key areas of policy.

Unfortunately, discussions of parental involvement rarely go beyond platitudes. One black researcher, Professor Sara Lightfoot, found that the relationship of family to school "was a topic largely ignored in the social science literature." [17] In her review of the literature, she concludes:

Schools will only become comfortable and productive environments for learning when the cultural and historical presence of black families and communities are infused into the daily interactions and educational processes of children. . . . The collaboration of black families and schools is the only hope for the successful schooling of black children.[18]

The question is: How does one define parental involvement? Comer, for example, was able to create a significant role
for parents in the schooling process that consisted of a "sharing of power," mainly over personnel. The most radical reform proposed during the school reform of the 1960s was
community control (with which I was associated). In that
concept, *formal* roles for involvement by low income parents
were created through elected school boards in the large cities. These school boards were to be comprised mostly of parents with children in the schools. The underlying concept was
to build into a system those representatives who had the most
to gain in formulating school policy. And these parent-
dominated school boards would establish policy over budget,
personnel, and curriculum—the three key areas of school policy.

Where there has been significant parental involvement, there
appear to have been educational gains. Lightfoot records improvement in reading scores where parents in a large urban
school system drew up contracts of participation.[19] Comer and
the *Phi Delta Kappan* study also show recorded gains.

Perhaps the most substantive study of parental involvement is that conducted by Marilyn Gittell, myself, and colleagues and published in the early 1970s. This study, *Local
Control in Education*, observed the dynamics of the only
community control experiment in a large school system. It
shows that when low income parents are provided with opportunities to effect change, they will respond favorably. For
example, an average of 25 percent of low income parents voted
in the school elections in the three boards with community
controlled schools; this compares favorably with the participation of middle-class parents in the suburbs.[20] In our study,
the typical board member was female, a high school graduate, a paraprofessional or poverty worker, and a public school
parent.[21] Most school board members are male and professional, and fewer are public school parents.[22]

Boards under community control spent nearly three-fourths
of their time on policy matters, whereas studies of suburban
boards show them to be predominantly occupied with lesser
housekeeping decisions.[23] The reason for this discrepancy

should be obvious. In the urban ghettoes, parents perceive the public schools to be failing them and want educational change. In the suburbs, parents are satisfied with the progress of the schools and seek to maintain the status quo.

Educationally, the community controlled districts proved to be highly innovative. Within a short period there were more varied and exciting programs in the Ocean Hill-Brownsville school district than in any comparable location in the country. Moreover, the I.S. 201 district in Harlem showed the only noticeable gains in reading in New York City—when the rest of the city school districts showed a decline.[24] The one great lack of these community controlled districts was that they had no general philosophy of education. But that disadvantage is not unique since most American schools seem to operate without a clearly defined philosophical orientation.

These experiments disprove the adage of critical teachers and observers that poor people are too ignorant to run city schools.[25] Not only did these low income parents perform responsibly—and in many cases imaginatively—but they were able to restore a much-needed and sorely missed hope for urban schools. Our study revealed, for example, that black youngsters in the fifth, sixth, and seventh grades had a better image of themselves as a result of the experiment and better attitudes toward school and life chances—a variable that Coleman found essential in *Equality of Educational Opportunity*. Unfortunately, these imaginative districts were eliminated and a weak decentralization law passed by the New York State legislature as a result of the efforts of the teachers' union.

In summary, only two of the variables associated with effective schools—parental participation and time on task—lend themselves to direct control through policy initiatives. The role of the principal is much too ethereal as of yet to be noticeably molded by public policy. And the heightening of teacher expectations rests with the development of a new consciousness among teachers toward the potentialities of poor students to achieve.

Perhaps the most important factor that has been overlooked by proponents of effective schools is student motivation. Certainly, the degree of student motivation has strong implications for learning. Only James Comer alludes to an increase in student motivation in his efforts to restore trust and confidence in urban schools. It is a variable that has not been directly considered in the research on effective schools, and it is the one factor that critics will cite as being absent in the research on effective schools.

Although consideration of student motivation shifts the focus from *what* the school does to the client, it is still important to scrutinize. What the school does has an effect on student motivation. In my experience in urban classrooms, first as a public school teacher a generation ago and then as a participant observer in the 1960s and 1970s in New York City, my strongest impression has been that many poor black youngsters lacked motivation. They did not seem deficient in intelligence; indeed, many were extremely intelligent in a "streetwise" sense. This lack of student motivation appeared to derive from a strong sense of alienation from the school and what it represents. An indication of alienation from what have been called "fortress schools" in the ghettoes is their constant defacing through graffiti and vandalism.

What accounts for this alienation? Most observers attribute the hostility of poor black youngsters to feelings of hopelessness. Reared in poverty, they perceive little opportunity to escape their situation either because of racism and discrimination or because of poor economic circumstances. Black teenage unemployment in the 1970s and 1980s was reported to be near 40 percent. Many black youths perceive an escape from poverty to exist only through athletics, an avenue that affects only a tiny percentage of youth.

The middle-class teacher feels confronted with a significantly different life-style among the urban poor, one characterized by apathy and despair. (Eliot Liebow's classic description of the black poor in Washington, D.C. ghettoes reflects those conditions. Liebow was a participant observer for over a year in the early 1960s and wrote his famed study *Tally's Corner*.) Although this life-style among the poor is discernible, it is not sufficient to create a culture of poverty, independent of the mainstream culture. What is crucial to this life-style is economics—not race or culture. The research suggests that with the abolition of poverty, the life-style of the poor would change. The trouble with the concept of a culture of poverty, as noted in chapter 5, is that it implies that the poor, by and large, are responsible for their own situation. If one wants to get ahead, one can do so through savings, hard work, or study—so the argument goes. This thinking ignores the considerable amount of racial discrimination and limited opportunities for advancement.

On a smaller scale, ghetto youngsters quickly assess their chances to move ahead. They fail to perceive the school as anything but an oppressive force, operated by middle-class teachers and administrators who are too often repulsed by the poor. The school becomes a place for marking time. Educational critics have called urban schools custodial schools. Educators have not been able, for the most part, to break through the apathy and hopelessness of ghetto youngsters.

Although educators and psychologists agree that motivation is within the individual, some educators argue that motivation can be strongly influenced by external forces; namely, the school environment. One of these factors, of course, is teacher expectations. And, some educators contend, teachers, with parents' help, can look for activities that can hold their students' interest.

Professors James Garbarino and C. Elliot Asp discovered that the size of a school affects achievement. Reviewing the literature on size and achievement, they conclude:

Large schools promote universalistic (impersonal) conditions, whereas small schools can promote personalistic (personal) conditions. . . . In broad terms, school size can have an impact on the character development of the student. Specifically, large schools tend to exert a negative influence on the character development of most students by depriving them of important experiences in participatory roles. Such experiences are essential for effective socialization to adulthood and for social relations.[26]

The large schools are, unfortunately, mainly located in the cities. As in its efforts toward decentralization and community control, the educational-reform movement of the late 1960s

sought to personalize education. The main goal was to reduce sizes of districts. Now evidence exists to show that the
very size of the school affects motivation, personal development, and, in turn, achievement.

Garbarino and Asp point to small alternative schools like
Harlem Prep to underline their main contention. Garbarino
writes that:

The storefront academies (such as Harlem Prep) that exist in some
parts of the country have in many cases exhibited remarkable strength.
They are small, which leads to strength because it generates the social cohesion created when everyone is needed. They are clearly
special. . . . They tend to present students with a high level of both
support *and* demand, the optimal conditions for producing achievement motivation.[27]

In the final analysis, efforts to improve schooling through
attempts to operationalize the new research can only be judged
over time and as more insight through research is obtained.
Certainly, there is no reason to believe—until proven
otherwise—that the lessons of effective schools cannot be applied to the larger number of schools where poor youngsters
are faring badly. Despite the difficulties, the search to discover effective strategies to improve the schooling of the mass
of urban poor in our nation should and must continue.

Notes

1. Steward C. Purkey and Marshall S. Smith, "Too Soon to Cheer?
Synthesis of Research on Effective Schools," *Educational Leadership* (December 1982), p. 64.
2. Ibid., p. 66.
3. Lawrence W. Lezotte et al., *School Learning Climate and
Student Achievement* (Tallahassee: Florida State University, 1980),
p. 59.
4. Ibid., p. 61.
5. Ibid., p. 60.
6. Ibid.
7. James Comer, *School Power* (New York: The Free Press, 1980),
p. 235.

8. Ibid., p. 128.

9. Robert Benjamin, *Making Schools Work* (New York: Continuum, 1981), p. 71.

10. Albert Shanker, "Teaching Is More Than Media Hype," *New York Times*, March 7, 1982, p. E7.

11. Ibid.

12. Arthur Blumberg and William Greenfield, *The Effective Principal* (Boston: Allyn & Bacon, 1980), p. 25.

13. Michael Rutter et al., *Fifteen Thousand Hours* (Cambridge, Mass.: Harvard University Press, 1979), p. 14.

14. National Center for Education Statistics, *Digest of Education Statistics 1982* (Washington, D.C.: U.S. Government Printing Office, 1983), p. 97.

15. *New York Times*, July 20, 1981, p. 1.

16. Ibid., April 10, 1983, p. 44.

17. Sara Lightfoot, *Worlds Apart: Relationships Between Families and Schools* (New York: Basic Books, 1978), p. 12.

18. Ibid., p. 175.

19. Ibid., p. 174.

20. Marilyn Gittell with Maurice R. Berube et al., *Local Control in Education* (New York: Praeger, 1972), p. 10.

21. Ibid., p. 15.

22. Ibid.

23. Ibid., p. 30.

24. Ibid., p. 112.

25. Martin Mayer, *The Teachers Strike* (New York: Harper & Row, 1969), p. 118.

26. James Garbarino and C. Elliot Asp, *Successful Schools and Competent Students* (Lexington, Mass.: Lexington Books, 1981), p. 112.

27. Ibid., p. 99.

PART
TWO: Effective Schools in Cuba

5
EDUCATION IN CUBA: AN OVERVIEW

We have examined and analyzed the few successes of effective schooling, mainly in the United States. One vital question arises: What can be learned from socialist systems pertaining to an urban poor and schooling? Socialist countries profess to have eliminated poverty, a problem that still plagues capitalist countries. Moreover, the élan of socialism may offer a different perspective toward schooling. There are indications that socialist societies may have success in effectively educating low-income students. For example, the Soviet Union has seen more of its peasantry enter higher education in the last two decades.[1]

Cuba, a nation of some 9 million people, was selected as the country to examine for three major reasons. First, Cuba has placed education as one of its highest priorities in the Revolution. Education is decreed to be a right under the Cuban constitution. Second, the Cuban Literacy Campaign was the only successful educational venture of the kind in recent memory. Third, Cuba has a large black population, approximately one-third, which corresponds to the black population in the urban areas of the United States. And that black population comprised the poorest sector prior to the Revolution. Had the investigation been made of the Soviet Union or the Republic of China, urbanologists in the United States might claim those experiences were not pertinent to that of the United States. But Cuba is an underdeveloped nation with many of the economic problems of such countries, and it has made a conscious effort to develop an educational system that will help the national economy.

Moreover, some observers of socialist countries have found Cuba to have had the least pathological symptoms of poverty since the Revolution. For example, the anthropologist Oscar Lewis suggested in the mid-sixties that certain societies lack a culture of poverty—a subculture that is characteristic of many low income groups and includes social pathologies such as crime and mental illness.[2] This subculture is further characterized by the absence of political participation in social institutions, lack of organization, the absence of childhood, and individual feelings of hopelessness. An academic debate ensued that questioned whether such a life-style or subculture was self-perpetuating. Critics contended that the chief problem of the concept of a culture of poverty was that it seemed to blame the victims—the poor—for their life-styles.

Nonetheless, Lewis surmised that certain societies, although having poor, did not display a culture of poverty. Chief of these were socialist countries, Cuba in particular. Writing in 1966 in La Vida a study of Puerto Rican poverty, Lewis concluded that "on the basis of my limited experience in one socialist country—Cuba—and on the basis of my reading, I am inclined to believe that the culture of poverty does not exist in the socialist countries."[3]

In the late 1960s, Premier Fidel Castro invited Lewis to conduct a study of poverty—named the Cuba Project—in the new socialist state. Lewis had examined poverty prior to the Revolution in a minor study, and he was anxious to perceive the present conditions of low income groups in Cuba. Unfortunately, part of the study involved interviewing a counterrevolutionary citizen who possessed sensitive personal information regarding a high government official, and the three-year study was cut short by the Cuban government. Shortly thereafter, Lewis died, but not before he recorded some thoughts on the Revolution's impact on the poverty culture. Lewis concluded, "I believe that I was overly optimistic in some of my earlier evaluation about the disappearance of the culture of poverty under socialism. However, there seems to me no doubt that the Cuban Revolution has abolished the conditions which gave rise to the culture of poverty."[4]

There is a lack of hard evidence to show that family background was a chief influence in educational achievement before the Revolution. Indeed, the educational scholarship is rather scant. (One must keep in mind also that in the United States, experimental and quasi-experimental research in education only really began to flourish in the 1960s, with increased financial support from the federal government.) There are several reasons for the dearth of such scholarship in Cuba. For one thing, most university graduates prior to the Revolution were lawyers and other professionals; after the Revolution, they were engineers and agricultural technicians. For another thing, the U.S. boycott of Cuba inhibited American scholars from conducting studies. Consequently, there does not exist a Cuban equivalent of the Coleman Report, or any such sophisticated and intensive study.

Nevertheless, there are still indications that prior to the Revolution, education was largely influenced by the socioeconomic background of parents. Dominguez shows that before the Revolution, school enrollments increased when times were good. Parents would have their children work during hard times rather than send them to school.[5] (Schools prior to the Revolution were both public and parochial.)

Since the Revolution, only three books have been written by American writers about some aspect of Cuban education. All three authors are enthusiastic about Cuban educational experiments, but none concentrates specifically on low income students and effective schooling. Two books were written by teacher-journalists and one by a professor of education, all of whom spent varying amounts of time in Cuba, from a few months to a year.

The first book on day care in Cuba—*Children Are the Revolution: Day Care in Cuba*—was written by Marvin Leiner, a professor of education at Queens College. Leiner provides a good description of the goals of Cuban education and the institution of day care. His book profits from his stay in Cuba for a year in the late 1960s, and he has an intimate knowledge of the schools since his three children attended Cuban elementary, junior high, and high schools respectively. Karen Wald, a teacher-journalist, spent eight months in Havana in the late sixties and made repeated visits in the seventies. Her book *Children of Che: Childcare and Education in Cuba* (1978) lacks analysis but does provide sufficient reportage of a neglected educational area. Jonathan Kozol's reevaluation of the Great Literacy Campaign, *Children of the Revolution: A Yankee Teacher in the Cuban Schools* (1978) is the best of the three books. Kozol provides analytical depth and brings superb teacher's skills to his task. As a result, his book on the Literacy Campaign is a classic in educational literature.

Education Prior to the Revolution

Before the Revolution, education was a happenstance affair. Although schooling was compulsory from 1900 on for students from the ages of six to fourteen, not all students attended.[6] In 1907, slightly over 30 percent of children aged five to fourteen attended school; by 1919, 28.7 percent were in school. A high of 63 percent was reached in the prosperous years 1925–1926.[7] As has been noted, the pattern for school attendance fluctuated with the island's economy. There are no statistics for the 1930s, but after a depression and a world war, the total was 58.1 percent in 1950. By 1955, that had dropped to 51 percent, the lowest in Latin America (excepting three countries).[8]

Literacy in Cuba also varied. In 1899, 43.2 percent of the population over ten years old was literate, and by 1931 literacy had reached 71.7 percent of the population.[9] This spurt in literacy and schooling in the beginning of the century was attributed to the first United States occupation.[10] Immediately prior to the Revolution, 76 percent of the population could read and write; this was one of the highest rates in Latin America but a sad figure nonetheless.

In 1953, over half the school-aged population had never attended school at all. Only 1 percent had completed a professional school, and less than 2 percent were in pre-university high schools.[11] Only 21,000 or one-half of 1 percent, had a university education.[12] Of these most were lawyers and arts graduates in a country where the economy was agricultural. There were only twenty-four hundred engineers. As a result, agriculture sorely lacked the necessary educated manpower to create a diversified economy not wholly dependent on sugar.

Still doctors, dentists, pharmacists, and nurses were in abundance, although most were located in Havana. There was a maldistribution of health professionals with the rural areas in dire need of practitioners. Teachers were plentiful although graft and corruption were rampant in their ranks. The main need was for engineers and agricultural technicians.

Expenditures for education rose significantly in the decade and a half from 1940 to 1956 although they were nowhere near the levels today. In 1940, the Ministry of Education spent $11,400,000, and in 1956 this increased to $74,300,000.[13] These were fairly respectable expenditures for the time.

Nonetheless, education in Cuba in the pre-Revolutionary era was characterized by ineffectiveness, dishonesty, and corruption. In Battista's time, this was especially true. Too much money was spent on central administration, and jobs were subject to graft. Indeed, some teachers hired substitutes to perform their work at lower pay.

Social Impact of the Revolution

The Cuban economy depends largely on the harvesting of sugar. Before the Revolution, there was substantial poverty, both rural and urban. The Revolution has raised the standard of living; 1970 estimates were that unemployment had fallen to 1.3 percent from 8.8 percent in 1962.[14]

The emphasis of the new government in social programs was on education and health. There had been a terrible misallocation of health care resources in pre-Revolutionary days. A United Nations study in the late 1970s shows that health care and facilities were not available for the mass of the population and that approximately 63 percent of all doctors were situated in Havana, which had but a third of the population.[15] The average income of doctors in urban areas was sixteen times that of those in rural areas, and only one-fourth of the doctors treated the poor, on a somewhat sporadic basis.[16]

Most important, the emphasis of the pre-Revolutionary health care system was on curative rather than preventive medicine. Just prior to the Revolution, mortality and morbidity rates of such chronic diseases as typhoid, malaria, gastroenteritis, diptheria, polio, and tetanus were exceptionally high. Yet there was no continuing program of prevention. The UNCTAD study states that "in part, this reflected the private enterprise character of the health system."[17]

The new Revolutionary leadership was fortunate enough to have recruited a number of physicians (in addition to Dr. Ernesto "Che" Guevara) and consequently there was acute interest in revamping the health system. The result was that medicine was socialized and access to a national free medical system made available, with the first beneficiaries being the poor. However, a mass exodus of doctors in the five years after the Revolution witnessed nearly one-half the total leaving Cuba, mostly for the United States.[18] The task of creating greater access was thus initially hampered by the lack of qualified physicians.

The impact of the Revolution on health care was dramatic. Chronic diseases such as polio were brought under control, and the death rate decreased to a respectable level. The ten leading causes of death in Cuba now resemble those of a developed country. The UNCTAD study concludes that "the health of the average Cuban has improved during the nearly two decades that have elapsed since the coming to power of the revolutionary government."[19] The study notes that the health of Cubans was also intimately affected by broad social economic changes caused by the Revolution. The only negative note in the UNCTAD study is that the Cuban system would not be recommended for other underdeveloped countries because of the cost.

It is still unclear how much impact the Cuban Revolution has had on eliminating racism in a nation with one-third of its population black. One black American scholar, Johnnetta B. Cole, has concluded that "racism, in its institutionalized forms" no longer exists, although "as expressed in attitudes and periodic behavior," it has not disappeared.[20] Writing in *The Black Scholar*, she defines "institutionalized forms of

racism" as "disproportionate unemployment among black
people; easier access to social services of health and education and decent housing for whites than for blacks; exclusion
of black people from decision making positions solely on the
basis of their race."[21]

Cole's analysis shows that the Revolutionary government has
waged a vigorous campaign against racism. Through procla-
mations, laws, and education, the Cuban government has been
on record against racial discrimination. Beaches, hotels, and
restaurants were opened to blacks. The primer used in the
Great Literacy Campaign, *Alphebeticemos*, contains a theme
on the origin of racial discrimination and the need to eliminate it. Most important, the socialist government's institution
of full employment directly aided the more than 700,000 job-
less, the majority of whom were black.[22] Universal education
gave blacks the schooling previously denied.

There is a dispute over how well the Cuban government
has been able to reduce institutionalized racism. One critic,
Jorge Dominguez, maintains that the leadership of the Revolution, circa 1965, was largely white with only 9 percent of
the Communist party membership black, and that blacks were
underrepresented in the army in the early 1970s.[23] Cole re-
plies that blacks are increasingly represented beyond their
percentage of the population in medical schools, in municipal assemblies, and throughout Cuban society. She expects that
a larger representation of blacks will be seen in the future in
the army and Party leadership. According to Cole, what racism exists seems to be on a personal, not institutional, level
and is a remnant among older Cubans from pre-Revolutionary
days. Even the more hostile observers admit that institutionalized racism in education is a thing of the past.

An American black attorney, Joel Dreyfuss, visited Cuba
with the American National Conference of Black Lawyers in
the late 1970s. He reported considerable progress in eliminating racism institutionally in Cuba, but he indicated some
problems remained. Dreyfuss found, for example, that "most
of the lawyers" were black, in their forties, and supporters of
the Revolution. According to one black Cuban lawyer, prior
to the Revolution, most black lawyers could not find work and

had to make a living in another profession. "The revolution," claimed this spokesman, "gave many of us the opportunity to work."[24]

On the other hand, a black American living in Cuba found no black race consciousness in Cuba or Third World countries. This black political exile felt that the American black rights movement was more advanced in its sensitivity to black issues. "Black Americans have such a developed sense of racial and political consciousness," he claimed, that "there's nothing like it in the Third World."[25] However, this exile may have mainly been a trifle homesick.

Education Overview Since the Revolution

The general educational system created by the Revolution resulted in a large increase in the number of students. Before the Revolution, only 60.8 percent of the school-age population attended school, 44.6 percent in primary and 28 percent in secondary.[26] Fifty percent in the countryside had no chance to attend school since there were no schools in the farthest areas. After the Revolution, the ministry committed itself to provide schooling to everyone so that teachers might be instructing as few as five or six students in remote rural areas until they could attend boarding schools in the country. In 1958–1959, there were only 4,563 graduates of secondary schools compared with 297,705 students in 1981–1982; there were 1,272 preuniversity graduates in 1958–1959 compared with 39,200 in 1981; only 3,100 students in the university in the earlier period compared with over 200,000 in 1983. In the 1983 year, there were 1.5 million primary school children, 1,700,000 intermediate students, and 200,000 higher education students. In 1982, 92.3 percent of students in the six-to-sixteen-year age range were attending school. For that year, the figures break down as 97.2 percent of primary school students aged six to twelve and 84 percent of students in the thirteen-to-sixteen age bracket.[27] The budget for education in 1957–1958 was 83,713,600 pesos; by 1982, that figure rose to 1,499,400,000 pesos.[28]

These changes in figures from pre-Revolutionary days are

dramatic. Equally dramatic are the qualitative changes. Before the Revolution, education was both public and private, with economic, social, and racial discrimination practiced. Wealthy parents sent their children to private schools, and the University of Havana would not admit anyone with Negro blood. One educational official recalls her first teaching assignment, in a thatched hut—which was not uncommon. The burgeoning construction of school buildings throughout Cuba has made that a pre-Revolutionary memory. Equally important, education in Cuba is now entirely free, a fact that officials, teachers, and principals constantly tell the visitor. This includes all food at boarding and semiboarding schools and snacks (usually taken twice a day).

The Cuban constitution specifically mandates that the state control and govern education, asserting that "education is a function of the state."[29] Education is a task in "which all society" participates.[30] There is a constitutional provision for parents and citizens to participate in education: This is to be accomplished "through the country's social and mass organizations, in the development of its educational and cultural policy."[31]

The Cuban constitution places some restriction on freedom of inquiry. Whereas scientific and scholarly inquiry are free, works of art must not be "contrary to the revolution."[32] That often translates into a prohibition of books with racist points of view or which "exaggerate violence and cruelty and horror" as well as those with antisocialist political views.[33] Such a stringent political conception often filters into a running of the schools. Marvin Leiner, for example, observed that the selection of school principals was often dependent on their " 'political history', i.e., dedication to the revolution."[34]

The basic structure of the post-Revolutionary Cuban school system is quite extensive. There are day care centers for children from forty-five days to four years and a preschool for five-year-olds. The elementary or primary system runs from grade one to six for the six-to-twelve-year-old population. A basic secondary school for students in the seventh through ninth grades who are in the twelve-to-fifteen age bracket corresponds to our junior high schools. What we have in the United

States as high schools are divided in Cuba into preuniversity,
pedagogical schools, polytechnical institutes, and schools for
the fifteen-eighteen age bracket. The preuniversity students
then go on either to a one-year polytechnical institute or to
universities and higher institutes.

The most striking schools are those in the countryside, where
students combine study with work in the fields. These schools
provide all educational and residential facilities for students.
This work-study program is the best known feature of Cuban
education since the Revolution.

One educational goal accomplished by the Revolution is
access. And universal education has opened up possibilities
for those black and poor prior to the Revolution. Currently,
over 50 percent of university students are workers.[35] Che
Guevara declared in 1960 that the university needed "to paint
itself with black and mulatto faces and open its doors to
workers and peasants."[36]

The Cuban experience has pertinence to the American scene
since Cuba has a significant black population. As noted previously, blacks constitute one-third of the population in Cuba.[37]
Fidel Castro, the premier of Cuba, designated Cubans as an
"Afro-Latino people."[38] The Revolution brought education to
blacks, who were (like those in the United States) most likely
to be low income. One black scholar observed that in the
Castro Revolution, "When education was made totally free,
from the first grade through the university level, education
became a reality for black Cubans, those most consistently
denied decent education before the revolution."[39] The simi-
larities between blacks in Cuba prior to the Revolution and
those in the large urban centers where they predominate in
the United States are obvious.

There are some unique differences in the Cuban educational system as compared to that of the United States. Perhaps the most striking is the work concept, which serves two
purposes: to acquaint the student with the world of work and
to satisfy the manpower needs of the economy. All levels of
schooling are involved. At the primary level, students maintain a small garden, even in the cities. At the intermediate
level, students spend forty-five days in the countryside to

guarantee that crops—tobacco, coffee, fruit, and such—will be tended to. No secondary student is involved in cutting sugarcane, an arduous task.

Another singular aspect of Cuban education is the early and constant emphasis on historical and political development. This begins in day care centers, where the older children have small corners reserved for historical events of the Cuban Revolution and the fight for independence from Spain. In the primary years, the history and political development of the country become an integral part of learning. In the ninth grade, the history of Cuba is taught. In preuniversity high school, the student studies liberation movements, Communist movements, and the struggles of different peoples for their freedom. In the twelfth grade, 160 hours of Marxism-Leninism is provided for.[40] Thus, revolutionary historical material is emphasized from the earliest years. In the United States, American history and later civics would correspond to the Cuban experience.

Another difference is the emphasis on foreign languages. Russian and English are taught, beginning at the intermediate level. The top 30 percent of students study Russian, and the lower 70 percent pursue English. In my visit to Cuba in the spring of 1983, my interpreter, Juan Jacomino, provided a testimonial of the study of English. He was not only expertly fluent in English, but he had never studied in an English-speaking country; his English was wholly learned in Cuban schools.

Cubans have a system of what they call boarding and nonboarding schools. The boarding schools are located in the countryside; they are residential schools where the students sleep during the week, returning home on the weekends. What they term semiboarding school is more of what we in the United States would call a day care system. Students spend the entire day until approximately 7 P.M. at school. They eat lunch there and participate in after-school activities of both an academic and a recreational nature. These semiboarding schools enable parents to work and have their children cared for until they can bring the children home. An aim of educational policy is to significantly increase the semiboarding primary schools throughout the country, a policy reflecting the increasing number of families where both parents work.

In primary schools, the initial cycle, from the first to the fourth year, concentrates on reading, writing, and math. There is some history of Cuba and some sciences, but the latter are stressed more in the second cycle, from the fifth to sixth grades. In the fifth and sixth grades, a cycle of history and sciences begins, continuing through the ninth year. Ancient history and botany are taught in the fifth year; medieval history and biology in the sixth year; modern history and zoology in the seventh year; contemporary Caribbean history and anatomy in the eighth year; and history of Cuba and physics in the ninth year.

There are also "special" schools for students with physical and mental problems, including the blind, deaf, and mentally retarded. Prior to the Revolution, these students did not receive any education. Officials maintain that a goal of educational policy is to increase the number of these schools.

One important pedagogical requirement in Cuban schools is a rigorous, comprehensive policy on homework. In the primary schools, for example, required homework is not only varied but intensive. First graders must spend between an hour and an hour and one-half; fifth and sixth graders must spend two hours.[41] Officials of some urban schools in the United States are now requiring mandated homework for various grade levels.

Beyond intermediate school, the Cuban school system is structured to offer high school for preuniversity training, technical schools for teacher training, technical institutes for accountants and the like, and polytechnical schools for skilled workers. At present, students must stay in school until they are seventeen years of age, so that some form of high school is necessary. Selection for these schools is based on a meritocratic system that takes interests into account. Students have a choice of sixteen academic requests, and they list, in order, their sixteen desired specialties. The Ministry of Education matches interest with academic class rank and assigns the student to a specific school.[42] The student is guaranteed a place at either a preuniversity, technical, or professional school. In order to attend medical school beyond college for example, students must have a consistent academic average of over 90 percent. As one official stated, however, "Only the best students at present go onto the university."[43]

This meritocratic system is not seen as unfair by the participants and the Ministry of Education. Rather, it is deemed the most just of systems. As the deputy minister of education, Dr. Elisa Wong García, stated in an interview, "No one would dare to object" to the placements.[44] Indeed, the Cuban educational system is modeled to a large extent on that of Europe as well as on other socialist systems where education, through university and beyond, is free but based on academic achievement. In a society such as Cuba's, where economic resources are scant, such a system appears reasonable. However, in the United States, which has a more flexible system and which is a wealthier nation, a meritocratic-bound system would come under severe criticism.

Perhaps the most severe limitation of Cuban education is its meritocratic character, which severely limits mobility. For example, in 1977 it was decided for the first time that not all qualified students desiring to enter the university could be admitted. As a result, students were admitted to careers of their choice on the basis of their grades. Since the Revolution the emphasis had been on engineers and agrarian specialists to meet the nation's needs. Because career decisions are based on early performance, and entry to university is a function of grades, many youngsters are unable to go to college. In the United States, which has a system partly based on meritocracy and partly open, there are greater chances for youngsters who do not "shine" early in their schooling to go to college. Although studies show that most college students in the United States are from middle-class or affluent families, a minority are from the poor. They are able to enter low cost universities and enhance their economic and social mobility. Moreover, indications are that greater numbers in the United States make career changes, so that a meritocratic system that emphasizes early proficiency in one career path has little long-term value in a sophisticated industrial society.

Even sympathetic observers have criticized the meritocracy in the Cuban school system. A team of American university professors who visited Cuba in 1978 was struck by the "meritocratic approach." The American educators were somewhat dismayed that Cuba would encourage an "elitist" system despite the egalitarian rhetoric of socialism. They observed that "the more highly motivated and talented students are identified early and given strong encouragement and support."[45]

A long-time sympathizer of the Cuban educational experiment, Marvin Leiner also has been critical of the incipient meritocracy within the Cuban school system. Leiner wrote the first American book on Cuban day care education, *Children Are the Revolution*, after a yearlong stay in Cuba in the 1960s and repeated visits. Leiner observes that Cuban schools use neither intelligence tests nor ability grouping, making them free from educationally "tracking" students. Nonetheless, he feels that the new emphasis on tests and promotion rates may lead to "stultification of both teacher and student, with critical thinking and creativity supplanted by rote learning."[46] Moreover, Leiner is dismayed by the creation of elite Cuban specialized high schools begun in 1969.

Professor Rolland G. Paulson, who could be categorized as a political liberal sympathetic to the Cuban Revolution, scores the meritocratic principle in the new schools. According to Paulson, this was a "surprising elitist solution for what is undoubtedly an egalitarian society."[47] Unfortunately, Cuban schooling "continues to practice traditional concepts of academic selection, grade promotion, and individualistic competition."[48]

A more radical observer, Professor Samuel Bowles (who has critiqued American education as needing first a socialist system) echoes Paulson's observations. Bowles believes that the "elitist" implications of the pressure for early career choices damage the aim of a classless, egalitarian state. "Yet even in a socialist society," Bowles continues, "a school system which stratifies children at an early age on the basis of their measured abilities and likely future roles in the production process will tend to reproduce a class structure and a sense of hierarchy in the consciousness of its students."[49]

The conflict between meritocracy and an egalitarian classless society is the greatest criticism of the Cuban educational system. It is understandable that an underdeveloped nation, formerly an oppressed economic colony, would turn to an alternative that promises a quick and sure way toward developing the necessary technical manpower for economic growth. Bowles nonetheless expresses a guarded hope that "the elitist implications of a vocationally segregated or 'ability grouped' educational system need not be decisive if they are strongly countered in other areas of social policy."[50] Yet Bowles warns of the danger of extending the meritocratic concept, which would "threaten the egalitarianism of the revolution."[51]

Notes

1. Torsten Husen, "The Equality-Meritocracy Dilemma in Education," in *Education, Inequality, and National Policy*, ed. Nelson F. Ashline et al. (Lexington, Mass.: D. C. Heath, 1976), p. 4.

2. Oscar Lewis, *La Vida* (New York: Random House, 1966), p. xlix.

3. Oscar Lewis et al., *Neighbors: Living the Revolution* (Urbana, Ill.: University of Illinois Press, 1978), p. xlix.

4. Ibid., pp. 52–60.

5. Jorge I. Dominguez, *Cuba: Order and Revolution* (Cambridge, Mass.: Harvard University Press, 1978), p. 71.

6. Dudley Seers, ed., *Cuba: The Economic and Social Revolution* (Chapel Hill: The University of North Carolina Press, 1964), p. 170.

7. Dominguez, *Order and Revolution*, p. 25.

8. Seers, *The Economic and Social Revolution*, p. 170.

9. Dominguez, *Order and Revolution*, pp. 24–25.

10. Ibid.

11. Seers, *The Economic and Social Revolution*, p. 164.

12. Ibid., p. 165.

13. Ibid., p. 171.

14. Dominguez, *Order and Revolution*, p. 182.

15. United Nations, Committee on Technology and Development, *Health and Educational Technology in Cuba* (Geneva: United Nations, August 31, 1979), p. 42.

16. Ibid.

17. Ibid., p. 44.

18. Ibid., p. 45.

19. Ibid., p. 78.

20. Johnnetta B. Cole, "Race Toward Equality: The Impact of the Cuban Revolution on Racism," *The Black Scholar* (November–December 1980, pp 2–3.

21. Ibid., p. 15.

22. Ibid., p. 9.

23. Dominguez, *Order and Revolution*, p. 226.

24. Joel Dreyfuss, "Cuba: The Racial Dilemma," *Black Enterprise* (April 1980), p. 39.

25. Ibid., p. 40.

26. Interview with Merida Lopez, researcher, Ministry of Education, Havana, May 9, 1983.

27. Ibid.

28. Interview with Elisa Wong García, deputy minister of education, Havana, May 11, 1983.

29. *Journal of Reading* 25, no. 3. (December 1981), p. 223.

30. Ibid.

31. Ibid.

32. Ibid.

33. Karen Wald, *Children of Che: Childcare and Education in Cuba* (Palo Alto, Calif.: Ramparts Press, 1978), p. 253.

34. Leiner, "Two Decades of Change in Cuba," p. 212.

35. Center for Cuban Studies, *Cuba Update* 1, no. 6 (January 1981), p. 5.

36. UNCTAD, *Health and Educational Technology*, p. 30.

37. Cole, "Race Toward Equality," p. 17.

38. Ibid., p. 3.

39. Ibid., p. 9.

40. García interview, May 1983.

41. Interview with Magaly García Ojeda, director of primary schools, Ministry of Education, Havana, May 10, 1983.

42. Interview with Antonio Mosot, director of Extraschool activities, Ministry of Education, Havana, May 11, 1983.

43. Lopez interview, May 1983.

44. García interview, May 1983.

45. American Association of State Colleges and Universities, *Impressions of the Republic of Cuba* (Chicago: ERIC Document Reproduction Service, ED 185–895, November 1979), p. 5.

46. Leiner, "Two Decades of Change in Cuba," p. 212.

47. Rolland G. Paulson, *Pre-Conditions for System-Wide Educational Reform: Learning from the Cuban Experience* (Chicago: ERIC Document Reproduction Service, ED 128–250, April 1976), p. 4.

48. Ibid.

49. Samuel Bowles, "Cuban Education and the Revolutionary Ideology," *Harvard Educational Review* 41, no. 4 (November 1971), p. 498.

50. Ibid., pp. 498–99.

51. Ibid.

6
EFFECTIVE SCHOOLS
IN CUBA AFTER THE
REVOLUTION

Let us examine the Cuban educational record in terms of effectiveness. First, the Cuban emphasis on education was aimed at achieving "three fundamental goals that other governments, to varying extents, have regarded as conflicting in their own programs: social justice, economic growth, and the creation of socialist man (a better people)."[1]

The Literacy Campaign

What makes the Cuban experiment even more of a possible model is the success of the Literacy Campaign in 1961. The Cuban Literacy Campaign is the only successful major literacy campaign in underdeveloped countries. Since 1950, UNESCO attempted nearly two dozen literacy campaigns—all of which failed.[2] The Cuban success has to be reckoned with, keeping in mind Oscar Lewis's observations concerning a lack of a culture of poverty in socialist states. In the late 1970s, UNCTAD could conclude that "few countries in history have emphasized education as much as Cuba since 1959 when the revolutionary government came to power."[3]

By 1953, the illiteracy rate was 23.6 percent, a figure that some Castro critics have mentioned as not extremely high in comparison with other Latin American countries.[4] Nevertheless, that is not only a sad indicator of Latin American conditions but a deceptive figure. In 1953, half a million children in Cuba did not attend school, and in 1959, there were a million illiterates.[5] In the cities, illiteracy was 12.6 percent whereas in the countryside it was a huge 41.7 percent.[6] Moreover, there were masses of *underschooled* people: an estimated additional million were semiliterate.[7] An additional factor was that although 23 percent of the national budget was spent for education, corruption had impeded the flow of these funds to the schools. We have noted, for example, that some tenured lifetime teachers would hire unqualified substitutes to perform their tasks at lower pay.

The new government's first step was to mobilize a vast literacy program in 1961, shortly after the Revolution. Nineteen sixty-one was declared by the Castro government to be the "Year of Education." The entire nation was enlisted to eliminate illiteracy in all Cubans over fourteen. The immediate need was to find teachers to educate a "located" 979,207 illiterates.[8] Housewives, workers, and students supplemented the 34,772 regular teachers so that a total of 260,420 "new" teachers became available.[9] The publicity behind the campaign was enormous. Radio carried forty-five-second spots on the campaign approximately fifteen times a day.[10] Popular songs were written about the campaign, and posters were displayed. It must not be forgotten that the U.S.-sponsored invasion of Cuba, the Bay of Pigs, took place during this educational campaign. Nonetheless, the Year of Education had significant results. Illiteracy was reduced from over 25 percent to 3.9 percent of the nearly 7 million people of Cuba.[11] In the urban areas such as Havana, illiteracy went down from 9.2 percent to a mere 1.4 percent; in the provinces, the results were more dramatic, with Oriente going down from 35.3 percent to 5.2 percent.[12] In a celebration marking the end of the Year of Education, Castro proclaimed that "four and a half centuries of ignorance have been demolished."[13]

The literacy units were the foundation of the Literacy Campaign. They were sent to all provinces. The literacy unit was made up of a chief technical advisor who was a professional teacher, twenty-five volunteers, and fifty to sixty illiterates. Since the program was voluntary (despite the massive government campaign to learn to read), there were some illiterates who simply refused to take part. René Mujica recalls one such old man whom he "just couldn't convince . . . to study."[14] The Literacy Campaign, however, was conducted with great insight into human character. Realizing that many poor illiterates in the provinces might feel ashamed to attend formal classes, the government provided students to live inconspicuously with the families.

A testimonial to the Great Campaign was the creation of a Literacy Museum in Havana where all of the tests, application forms, questionnaires, and letters by former illiterates to Premier Fidel Castro are on display. It is indicative of the large role education plays in Cuba. The museum, situated in a large educational complex, is a small, well-kept bungalow that features a film on the Literacy Campaign and is the repository of its records and memorabilia. Included are the bayoneted blackboards of a teacher attacked during the Bay of Pigs uprising as well as the press clips from around the world congratulating the Cuban victory over illiteracy. One interesting clipping shows Premier Castro meeting a 106-year-old peasant woman who had just learned to read and write; she lived to be 117.

An interesting sidelight to the Literacy Campaign was how it was reported. UNESCO sent a team under the direction of Dr. Anna Lorenzetto, an Italian scholar, to study the campaign and its results. Dr. Lorenzetto's study was an enthusiastic and approving recognition of Cuba's efforts in eliminating illiteracy. However, the study has been unavailable since its publication in 1965. Jonathan Kozol suspects that this unavailability is due to the fact that the report proved embarrassing to UNESCO since Cuba's Literacy Campaign was the only such program not funded by UNESCO and "the only one that proved to be a real success."[15]

The UNESCO study, which is distributed by the Cuban Ministry of Education, conducted from February 27 to March 27, 1964, concludes that the Great Literacy Campaign involved the attainment of realizable goals. "The Campaign was not a miracle," the UNESCO team observes, "but rather a difficult conquest obtained through work, technique, and organization."[16] Most important, the Cuban experience had "an indicative value" that offers "examples of reading and writing to adults and adult education."[17] In conclusion, the UNESCO team viewed the Literacy Campaign as "a great event in the educational field that could serve as a model for other literacy campaigns."[18]

There were other less tangible results. The educational campaign sparked a mass interest in culture. In the 1970s, the American educator Jonathan Kozol interviewed teachers and students who had participated in the Great Campaign. One woman told him that her first act after learning to read at the age of seventeen in the Year of Education was to write Castro a letter. Her second act was "to begin to memorize my favorite poems," a habit she "learned during that year" and continues to follow."[19]

Why did the Cuban Literacy Campaign succeed where so many UNESCO attempts in underdeveloped countries failed? This is difficult to ascertain. The evidence suggests that the revolutionary fervor of a new nation undergoing profound social change to eliminate inequality dispelled large-scale despair and hopelessness among the poor.

The social, political, and economic change that took place during the Revolution swept motivation to a crest of initial high feeling, and the Literacy Campaign came shortly after the Revolution, when feeling was still intense. The comments of those interviewed by Jonathan Kozol indicate that many of the teachers, students, and education officials were carried away by the élan of the Revolution. Their enthusiastic participation in the Literacy Campaign was their contribution to the revolution.

Consider, for example, the testimony that Kozol offers of teachers in the Great Campaign:

As veterans of the literacy struggle reminisce today, it seems apparent that the basic, or at least, initial motivation had a lot to do with the desire of kids (most of them urban, many middle class) to share in an adventure which appeared in certain graphic ways to carry on the work-and-struggle-in-the-mountains symbolized by Che Guevara and Fidel. A kind of "ethical exhilaration," modeled upon these heroes, seems to have been the overwhelming impetus.[20]

Kozol documents these impressions through the statements of men and women who were teachers during the Great Campaign. One young lady recalls that her first motive "was not to teach" but "to be part of a great struggle . . . my first chance to take a stand."[21] A Cuban educator, Mier Febles, assessed the goal of the campaign to be larger than the narrow one of education; it was "always greater than to teach poor people how to read."[22] What happened was that "the peasants discovered the word" and "the students discovered the poor," and as a result, "together, they all discovered their own *patria*."[23]

A classic example of a political stance is that of René J. Mujica. Mujica, a university graduate, is presently with the Cuban Foreign Office in Washington. He recalled his experience as a twelve-year-old volunteer literacy teacher as "the most important single experience of my life."[24] Mujica underwent more of a political than an educational experience in the Great Campaign. His participation as a twelve-year-old city boy living with families in the poor rural provinces put him in contact "with a kind of poverty, a kind of reality which [he] could never have dreamed could exist in this world."[25] The result was that "the campaign played a role in awakening [his] political consciousness."[26] It became his political moment of truth.

The first evaluation (that of UNESCO) to be made of the Literacy Campaign shortly after it was conducted strongly notes the political overtones of the educational effort. The UNESCO team perceived that the campaign was "sustained by the revolutionary impulse" and could not be set apart from a political evaluation . . . due to the fact that the Campaign was, in itself, a political event."[27] The report observes that the sending of volunteers to the homes and provinces of the *campesinos* was a brilliant stroke. Perhaps the campaign could have been successfully waged through the radio and television media—that is, by having courses taught over the electronic media rather than by volunteers. But through intimate association with a volunteer, the *campesino* "has learned how to read and has become a revolutionary" (emphasis added).[28]

Another interpretation that complements the political effect thesis is that the pedagogy used in the Literacy Campaign resembled much of the Paulo Freire revolutionary pedagogy that was successful in Brazil in a smaller-scale literacy program in the 1960s. Freire had devised an educo-politics geared for the oppressed in authoritarian nations with social, political, and economic inequality. In his major work, *The Pedagogy of the Oppressed*, Freire outlines a teaching style and curriculum that seek *first* to make the oppressed aware of their condition so as to develop a sense of individual worth and dignity that would then propel them to political action. According to Freire, the oppressed must develop a political awareness of their condition before they can sufficiently master their resources to develop their learning potentials. Once victims truly perceive the cause of their affliction and the revolutionary course to change that condition, they are free to learn. This process Freire calls *conscientizio*:

Men who are bound to nature and to the oppressor in this way must come to discern themselves as *persons* prevented from *being*. And discovering themselves as *Pedro*, as *Antonio*, or as *Josefa*. This discovery implies a different conception of the meaning of designations: the words "world" "men," "culture," "tree," "work," "animal," reassume their true significance. The peasants now see themselves as transformers of reality (previously a mysterious entity) through their creative labor. They discover that, as men, they can no longer continue to be "things" possessed by others; and they can move from consciousness of themselves as oppressed individuals to the consciousness of an oppressed class.[29]

In his reexamination of the Great Campaign, Kozol notes that it possessed "an approach to literacy that is identified with Paulo Freire."[30] Kozol writes:

The Cubans, much like Freire's colleagues in Northeast Brazil, not only based their campaign on the search for charged and active (Freire calls them 'generative') words but also insisted upon a dialogical relationship between the teacher and 'the one who chooses to be taught.' Even the prior exploitation of a photograph or illustration suggests the simple drawings used by Freire's colleagues to initiate the learning process in Brazil.[31]

Freire's books became classics in educational literature much adapted throughout the world. One index of his influence was that the literacy program he directed in Brazil was so effective that he was exiled by the reigning dictatorship.

The Cuban teacher's manual, *Alfabeticemos* has chapters stressing the contrast between the old and new orders. Such themes as "The Land Is Ours," "The Right to a Home," and "Cuba Had Riches [but] Was Poor" illustrate the revolutionary condition.[32] Blending with the high fervor of the nation, such teaching and learning techniques seemed to have been the appropriate approach to a massive literacy campaign.

Whether the Cuban educational officials were thinking of a political effect or not, they were intent on making the gains of the Literacy Campaign permanent. For this reason, they revamped the old educational system and designed it to make the campaign "only the starting point for raising the cultural level of the Cuban people."[33] An adult education program was fashioned with the intent of raising the level of the new literates from the third to the sixth grade (the end of grammar school). The "Battle of the Sixth Grade" ensued, and after two years a test revealed that over 1 million adults were involved in it. Over half were at the level of the first two grades; nearly a quarter were at third- and sixth-grade level, and nearly 20 percent were at the level of secondary school.[34] Currently, seven-hundred-thousand workers are in adult education with four-hundred-thousand in primary, two-hundred-thousand in basic secondary, and one-hundred-thousand in preuniversity level.[35] Approximately nine-hundred-thousand adults are at the sixth-grade level in achievement.[36]

Early Setbacks

The success of the Literacy Campaign did not initially usher in a golden age in the Cuban schools. The first goal after the Literacy Campaign was access. And in that respect, the Revolution dramatically increased elementary school attendance from 55 percent of the age group prior to the Revolution to 100 percent by the 1970s.[37] By 1972, Castro could openly discuss the shortcomings of the school system. In a speech to the

Second National Congress of the Young Communist League, Castro revealed that the schools evidenced ineffectiveness. Using dated figures that went back to the mid-sixties (shortly after the Revolution), Castro claimed that half of the children in elementary were overaged grade repeaters.[38] He said that passing rates were worse for the rural schools than for the urban schools in primary grades: 11.7 percent of rural pupils graduated from the sixth grade whereas 34.2 percent graduated in urban schools (1965–1966 figures.)[39] At the junior high school level, only 13.6 percent graduated in 1966–1967.[40] That Castro cited these dated figures in a 1972 speech has been interpreted by one observer as evidence of a continuing problem faced by the Revolutionary government. It reinforces the theory that a political effect was part of the Literacy Campaign.

Castro placed much of the blame on poor student motivation. First, students weren't serious enough to envision careers that would bolster the Revolutionary economy: "There are few young people who are thinking about agricultural or industrial training. . . . There are 24,033 people studying languages. That's fine. We should be glad that so many people realize the importance of studying foreign languages. But who is going to produce the material goods in the future, and how?[41]

Equally important, the Revolutionary educational system had not yet created the "new socialist man," according to Castro in 1972. Perhaps exhorting more than criticizing, he lamented that "we still don't have the new man, and we no longer have the old one."[42] Castro complained that

the new man doesn't exist yet. . . . The irresponsible fellow that destroys equipment, who doesn't work or study is not yet a new man. The old man who lived under capitalism knew how hard it could be to find a job. He learned about discipline because life, the factory, and hunger imposed it upon him. When you arrive at a sugar mill today, you do not see this discipline. The discipline of the old man is gone and we don't have the new man with corresponding discipline . . . self-discipline and awareness of his obligations and tasks.[43]

There is some indication that in the early days of the Revolution, there was a strong relationship between education and poverty. For example, in *Children of Che*, Karen Wald describes a school that was situated in the midst of *solares* (poor tenements prior to the Revolution) where the promotion rates of students were not as high as at other schools. One student noted, "We have a pretty good promotion rate—although it could be better."[44] Another study conducted in the late 1960s as part of Oscar Lewis's aborted Cuba Project recorded a high rate of school dropouts in a relocated neighborhood that had once been one of Havana's worst slums. Douglas Butterworth notes that in this relocated neighborhood, only sixty-three of eighty-four children interviewed were attending school in the six-to-fourteen age group.[45] In sum, about one-fourth of children in this age group were not attending school. Butterworth concludes for this scant survey that "there were too many school dropouts, too many loafers, too few who really understood what the revolution was all about."[46]

Some critics have speculated that currently teachers are "socially promoting" students. Jorge Dominguez (who left Cuba with his family in 1960 at the age of fifteen and was refused permission to return to pursue his study of Cuban society) questions "whether teachers have simply been promoting unqualified students as a result of the politicization of the issue that resulted from the Prime Minister's complaints."[47]

There are, however, no social promotions as such in Cuban schools.[48] Students are promoted mainly on the basis of a standardized national examination given at the end of each educational level. In addition, periodic tests and daily monitoring are considered. In order to be promoted in elementary school, students must demonstrate sixth-grade competency. Students who graduate and have had difficulty are then channeled into vocational schools to learn a trade such as carpentry and plumbing. An academic track is provided for those who have done well in elementary school. In 1978, 81.7 percent of all junior and senior high school students were in an academic track.[49] The emphasis in recent years has been to improve the quality of teaching and education, and it will remain so in the near future.

Reform

The Cuban government took extraordinary measures in 1972 to instill student motivation and to address the needs of the economy. The system of rural boarding schools created previously was accelerated to house both urban and rural students. These students would work and study, in time to help the yearly harvest. Primary boarding schools were reserved for children "with social problems."[50] By the end of the 1970s, nearly a half-million students were in the countryside boarding schools. Primary school students work two hours a day and supply their own needs. Intermediate school students work three to four hours a day in agricultural production.

The emphasis shifted from urban education to rural education with a work-study format. A work-study counterpart system for urban schools has yet to be devised because of a difficulty in finding a suitable work component. The rural boarding schools now play a useful part in the economy. Some American observers, such as Professor Arthur Schlesinger, Jr., have criticized the work-study as involving child labor, a practice that would not be tolerated in the United States. The aim of the schools-in-the-country was clear, however. According to Abel Prieto Morales, the government was "looking for a formula by which the students could help the economy and *through which the students would develop good working habits*" (emphasis added).[51]

In order to achieve the turnaround, a complementary strategy was devised. The Cuban government initiated a large-scale restructuring of the educational system in 1975. The *"Perfeccionamiento* (the "Plan for Improving Schools") was begun in a five-year cycle. The emphasis was on increasing the quality of Cuban education. That restructuring involved revamping the elementary school into two stages; a first- through fourth-grade cycle and a fifth- through sixth-grade cycle. The first cycle stresses accomplishment in Spanish and mathematics. Biology, physics, chemistry, and mathematics are re-

quired courses in elementary school—all indicating the shift
to pre-engineering and agricultural career options. There are
no elective courses until grade eleven. In addition, the plan
revised all textbooks and teachers' manuals. The focus now
was on how well the schools performed in national examinations and promotion rates.

Minister of Education José R. Fernández believed that the
improvement of retention and promotion that characterized the
late 1970s and early 1980s in Cuban schools was directly at-
tributable to the perfecting plan.[52] Officials talked of the flow
of students through the triangle of education. In 1958, prior
to the Revolution, 88 percent of students were in primary
school, with 11 percent in intermediate school and 0.3 percent in higher education. At present, 54 percent are in primary, 40 percent in intermediate, and 6 percent in higher education.[53] Educational officials claim that the "big achievement
of the last decade is the flow of students through the system."[54] And the promotion rates have increased significantly.
Approximately 93 percent of primary school students graduate. In the intermediate schools, the figure is approximately
66–70 percent.[55] According to officials, "Cuba is one big
school."[56]

The major reason for the turnaround is the introduction of
a new teacher-student system that allows teachers to remain
with their charges during formative years. The primary school
is divided into two cycles—from the first grade to the fourth
grade, and the fifth and sixth grades. Under the perfecting plan,
teachers remain with their students from the first to the fourth
grade. The underlying educational philosophy is that teachers will better know the students' deficiencies and have more
time to work on these shortcomings. Students in the first four
years are thus promoted without regard to national or provincial tests. Minister of Education Fernández stated that the
"success of students is very closely linked to retention and
the ones who drop out have problems passing the course."[57]
He pointed out that when children repeat the early years, their
very size embarrasses them in front of smaller and younger
children, and they are intimidated and drop out.

In the fifth year, students are promoted on the basis of school

and provincial tests (60 percent of the promotion is dependent on school tests and 40 percent on a provincial test). In
the sixth year, graduation is predicated on a mark based 60
percent on school tests and 40 percent on a national examination. So there is not exactly social promotion in Cuban
schools: The fifth- and sixth-year promotions have external
criteria.

Other factors pertain to these reforms. For example, there
has been a decline in the birthrate as a result of an intensive
birth control campaign. In 1953, there were 173,313 births,
and shortly after the Revolution in 1965, a high of 267,611
births was recorded. In 1981, that figure declined to 136,211
as a result of the birth control campaign.[58] That results in a
smaller percentage to be attending primary school. And prior
to the Revolution, there was no family consciousness of what
study meant since many parents were illiterate. They rea-
soned that since they had only attended primary school, that
is all that would be required for their sons and daughters. Today, officials admit that they must educate parents who feel
that a primary school education is enough. Cuba now guar-
antees an education to all as far as their talent and motivation
will carry them. In consequence, one out of every three Cubans is studying today.[59]

The aim of Cuban educational policy is to produce an educationally developed nation. At present, the average educational attainment in Cuba is six years of primary. However,
policy makers hope to increase that average attainment by one
year after every three-year interval.[60] There are plans to make
school compulsory until the ninth grade in the near future
(although that has become a reality in effect), and in the not-
too-distant future to make school compulsory until the twelfth
grade.[61]

One key factor about school performance is that students
lack the alienation characteristic of pupils in American urban
schools. In my interviews with students, teachers, principals,
and officials from the Ministry of Education, I found discipline was not perceived as a serious problem. In the United
States, by contrast, discipline ranks as the number one concern among parents in annual Gallup polls in education and

is a serious problem in urban schools. School people in Cuba were rather amazed that such a question was posed.

That amazement characterized responses from elementary and junior high school students to the minister of education. Indeed, Mr. Fernández, who consented to be interviewed at the end of my visit to Cuban schools, and who was briefed on questions by an aide, was more emphatic in his answers. He pointed out that school discipline was at best a minor problem. What cropped up, as occasional unmolded behavior, was the "friskiness" of youth (such as an odd day missing school to swim on the banks of Malecón a practice he had also indulged in as a youth). Cuban schools were free from the type of alienated school behavior reported in the United States. He added that the Cuban society had "no drug, no crime and no gambling problems."[62]

One aspect of the Cuban school system that controls discipline problems is the close working of parent and student organizations. The Pioneers, a student run organization molded on the Soviet example, has as its major objective a monitoring of student academic performance and the handling of whatever discipline problems arise in schools. Promotion rates, student attendance, and student discipline are the chief concerns of the Pioneers. Should a student prove unruly or violate school discipline, he or she is talked to by the Pioneer leaders, and a system of peer pressure is exerted. This is also the case with the School Council, which is made up of a parent as president, delegates of parents from each class, and a delegate from the Cuban Women's Federation, the Committee for the Defense of the Revolution, and the Communist party. This School Council also concerns itself with the triad of promotion, attendance, and discipline. Should a student miss school, council representatives visit parents to find out the reason. Minor discipline problems are also handled by the School Council. Great stress is placed on promotion and attendance rates, and rewards and emoluments are forthcoming from the Ministry of Education. One such reward for schools with high attendance and promotion rates is fifteen days at the City of Pioneers, a huge educational and recreational facility on the beach on the outskirts of Havana.

There are also no signs of graffiti or marks of vandalism. For the most part, Cuban students are made aware of the need to take care of state property, including books and supplies, and there are few instances where this is not the case. Cuban students have no sense of the school as the enemy, as often is the case with ghetto students in U.S. urban schools.

Moreover, an infrastructure of parents and students exists in Cuba with the express aim of supporting the goals of learning. The Committees for the Defense of the Revolution (CDR) exist to aid the educational process, and nearly 8 percent of Cuban parents belong to CDR.[63] A program for model parents was established. These "exemplary" parents have to have a child with over a 95 percent attendance rate who studies regularly and passes all school courses. In addition, the parents must know school regulations, attend school meetings, and visit the school regularly. Slightly under one-fourth of all Cuban parents have been designated exemplary parents in recent years.[64]

At present, parental participation is advisory and somewhat similar in nature to that in parental organizations in the United States. However, in America most local school districts elect their school boards, giving them considerable power over school policy. In Cuba, there are School Councils affiliated with every school whose main duties are to cooperate with the schools. These involve everything from making sure that students do their homework and attend classes each day to having parents contribute services on a voluntary basis. The parents are not allowed to criticize teachers or voice any dissatisfaction directly. According to Vice-Minister of Education Abel Prieto Morales, "That is the job of the inspectors and technicians."[65] In short, parents do *not* form an independent bloc to counterbalance school professionals and the government. For that matter, parents really do not exercise power for the most part in the United States. But the potential in the United States for strong, effective parental participation exists.

The student organization the Pioneers completes the student-parent infrastructure. The Pioneers, to which approximately 90 percent of the students belong, help run the schools.

Students participate in decisions apart from key school policy such as curriculum, budget, and personnel and set goals and standards for their peers. One Pioneer official described the aim of the student group: "Why do we have an organization? Well, look at what we are trying to do. We are trying to form future communists. We want a complete person, a communist in practice, a person with an integral education, not just a technician or scientist or artist."[66]

A subsidiary result was to create tremendous group consciousness among students. In *Two Worlds of Childhood*, his classic study of Soviet and American early education, Professor Urie Bronfenbrenner documents this development of "collective socialization." The student youth group sought to have students be "diligent, study well, like school, and respect grown-ups."[67] Moreover, "the aims and values of these organizations," Bronfenbrenner writes, "are of a piece with those promulgated for the school program itself."[68]

Sometimes these young Pioneers become overzealous. In the Soviet Union, one youngster denounced his father as a collaborator.[69] An American journalist quotes a Cuban Pioneer official as relating an incident where the young Pioneers "transformed the conduct of their parents."[70] In this instance, a young Pioneer shamed his father into staying in Cuba when he wanted to emigrate by saying that his father was betraying his country.

What we see in early school socialization of youngsters in the United States, according to Bronfenbrenner, is an over-reliance on individualism. In socialist countries, the opposite is true: Youngsters become overly group conscious. The conclusion one derives from reading Bronfenbrenner's study is that there should be a balance between the two social, political, and cultural systems in this regard.

Much emphasis has been placed by the Ministry toward upgrading the teaching profession. One indication of that effort to obtain quality with the perfecting plan reforms has been the easing of the acute teacher shortage and the upgrading of teacher education. In the first few years of the Revolution, the need for staff was so severe (since most teachers emigrated to the United States) that some teachers were taking morning classes to learn what they were to teach the same afternoon.[71] In addition, materials were in such short supply that there were not sufficient textbooks. At present, all primary school teachers have earned teaching diplomas, and admissions requirements have been upgraded for teachers at all levels of public schooling.[72] Before the Revolution, the teacher-student ratio was one teacher for every forty-three pupils; by the mid-seventies, that ratio had been nearly halved to one teacher for every twenty-three students.[73]

The teacher shortage that severely plagued the Cuban schools originated due to conflicting factors. First, a commitment to expansion and universal education in Cuba created a sharp demand for trained teachers. Second, the exodus of middle-class professionals shortly after the Revolution compounded the problem. And third, the existing teacher ranks at the time of the Revolution were plagued by corruption and the hiring of unqualified substitutes. The most important decision was whether to expand despite the lack of qualified professionals. The Cuban government decided to expand schooling; subsequently, the emphasis has been on improving teacher quality.

A number of efforts have been made to improve teacher quality. In 1972, prospective students at teacher-training institutes had to have a ninth-grade level of achievement (up from the sixth grade); by 1977, a twelfth-grade education was required for admission for teachers of intermediate education.[74] By the beginning of the Five Year Plan in 1975, 46.8 percent of primary school teachers had not yet received diplomas, although most were in process. By 1978, nearly three-fourths had obtained teaching diplomas.[75] Leiner observed that in one school he visited in the provinces in 1979, forty of the sixty teachers were licensed whereas the remainder were still in training.[76] Although the Cuban system has improved in the number and training of teachers, there is still a lack of qualified instructors. One indication of the emphasis on obtaining teachers is that an academic high school teacher may earn more than a beginning physician.[77] Cuban officials continue to cite the obtaining of teachers and upgrading of their training as the biggest problem in Cuban schools.

Part of the success of the reform must be attributed to changing student and national attitudes concerning the creation of the "new socialist man." Ernesto "Che" Guevara had sounded the key for the development of the "new socialist man." The "ultimate and most important revolutionary aspiration," Guevara wrote, was "to see man liberated from alienation."[78] The "new socialist man" would be compassionate, considerate of others, and free from the evil effects of competition. It was a heroic ideal, and it placed a huge burden on the schools as the chief national cultural institution. According to Castro, the school will play a crucial role:

We expect this school will form such a kind of citizen. We expect a great spirit of fraternity among the students. The development of a collectivist mentality. Egotism and individualism will be systematically combatted. . . . [While the society] will produce a man linked in human brotherhood. The most fraternal spirit shall prevail among students, the largest possible cooperation from the stronger towards the weaker, from those with greater dexterity in studies towards those who have less. This is the true brotherly spirit of cooperation, of help.[79]

Perhaps socialist consciousness has now deeply permeated youth. In his conversations with Cuban students in the late 1970s, Jonathan Kozol found evidence that the development of the "new socialist man" was at hand. One student, Leonora, cited concern for others—the welfare of society—as being the chief determinant of a career. Although she "would deeply wish" to dance and sing and to perform on stage, she opted for a career as a teacher of performers since "it is my obligation in the revolution," teachers being in short supply.[80]. Kozol observes that the "sense of obligation to 'the others'—or, as some say it, 'in the revolution'—is an overriding theme in almost every conversation of this kind."[81]

Another factor influencing scholastic performance is the introduction of "interest circles." These interest circles in Havana cover 206 different academic specialties tied in with twenty-three branches of the economy. The interest circles, which range from agricultural and industrial specialties to literary and artistic ones, are designed to further academic competence in areas that may best serve the development of the economy. Students visit the Pioneer Palace in Havana in September and choose a specialty. (They have a month to change their minds and select another one.) Eighteen state departments are linked with the interest circles which provide the raw material and instructors to the Pioneer Palace, and these agencies are responsible to the Council of State, the highest governing body in Cuba.

Information concerning the interest circles is disseminated through the mass media and by personnel visiting schools to tell students of their range of activities. The students pursue the interest circles in the afternoon when they are performing after-school activities. (Four and a half hours per day are allocated for learning instruction in Cuba urban primary and intermediate schools. The afternoon is reserved for reinforcement activities.)

Students in interest circles receive further intensive experience with working professionals in the Pioneer Palaces, which they visit once a week. (There are fifty-nine such palaces in Cuba.) The Ernesto "Che" Guevara Pioneer Palace, built in 1979, that I visited is typical. It handles 1,717 Pioneer interest circles on a two-session-a-day basis and has thirty-thousand Pioneers receiving vocational orientation. The palace enrollment had 45-percent primary students and 55-percent secondary students with groups ranging from ten to thirty Pioneers.[82] Some interest circles that I observed included craft design by intermediate students. In the latter class were three students who were deaf but could read lips, and they were included in an experimental project to have more handicapped participate in palace activities with interest circles.

Activities are determined to a large extent by the proximity of industry and agricultural enterprises. In Havana, there were not that many agricultural interest circles because of the urban character of the economic enterprises. The aim of interest circles, then, is to provide a complementary function to Cuban education, develop other phases of student personality, and help students toward possible career choices. In short, interest circles provide a strong academic reinforcement to traditional learning in Cuban schools.

In addition, school personnel and educational officials strongly believed that students have the capacity to learn at least a basic minimum. "All children have the possibility of learning," Magaly García Ojeda, director of primary schools, maintained, "although some take longer."[83] She felt that the aim of Cuban education was for "all children to have an educational minimum."[84] However, as has been mentioned, the Cuban educational system, meritocratically controlled, does not provide for all students to become college graduates. Education officials do not believe that all children have the capacity to enter the university.

Another reason officials believe school effectiveness has increased, especially in the primary years, has been the introduction of a phonics approach to reading. In developing the perfecting plan during the 1970s, curriculum specialists reviewed the relevant research and chose the phonic analytic synthetic method, originated in the Soviet Union and still used in that country.[85] It differs from other phonics approaches. A Soviet linguist, Lev Vygostky, discovered that some languages, like Chinese, are not dependent on an auditory factor in their writing systems. On the other hand, some languages, such as Spanish and English, are linked to hearing.[86] This method emphasizes comprehension of written as well as oral language through sound structure.

In summary, the Cuban educational experience has been fairly effective. First, Cuba was successful in raising the literacy level of its pre-Revolutionary poor. Second, Cuba has been effective at the primary level and, increasingly, at the intermediate level in educating post-Revolutionary generations. The reasons for the latter success are many and varied. A structural reform that included schools in the countryside with a work ethic infused student motivation. Then the Ministry of Education consistently upgraded teacher education. There was a revamping of the reading method and a cycling of elementary teachers to accompany the same class through the first four years to correct deficiencies. Most important, an infrastructure of parents and students contributed to student motivation. And lastly, it appears that teachers and school personnel have reasonably high expectations of students. These last two variables coincide with conclusions of the research on effective schools for the urban poor in capitalist societies.

But perhaps the most important ingredient in the educational recipe is the substantial elimination of poverty in this Communist state. Professor Lewis found that Cuba had abolished the conditions that gave rise to a culture of poverty. Nevertheless, the educational task was not an overnight success. Over half a million of mostly middle-class citizens emigrated from Cuba after the Revolution, leaving the schools with the descendants of a formerly poor class. As Douglas Butterworth points out, this strata of Cuban society was slow to comprehend the magnitude of the Revolution.[87] In time, however, Cuban students became more motivated as the school setting was reformed to permit greater success.

Notes

1. United Nations Committee on Technology and Development, *Health and Educational Technology in Cuba* (Geneva: United Nations, August 31, 1979), p. 2.

2. Jonathan Kozol, *Children of the Revolution: A Yankee Teacher in the Cuban Schools* (New York: Delacorte Press, 1978), p. 72.

3. UNCTAD, *Health and Educational Technology*, p. 2.

4. Abel Prieto Morales, "The Literacy Campaign in Cuba," *Harvard Educational Review* 51, no. 1 (February 1981), p. 31.

5. Ibid., pp. 31–32.

6. Ibid., p. 32.

7. UNCTAD, *Health and Educational Technology*, p. 4.

8. Ibid.

9. Morales, "The Literacy Campaign in Cuba," p. 37.

10. UNCTAD, *Health and Educational Technology*, p. 7.

11. Ibid., p. 9.

12. Ibid.

13. Morales, "The Literacy Campaign in Cuba," p. 38.

14. René J. Mujica, "Some Recollections of My Experiences in the Cuban Literacy Campaign," *Journal of Reading* 25, no. 3 (December 1981), p. 223.

15. Kozol, *Children of the Revolution*, p. 75.

16. United Nations Educational, Scientific and Cultural Organization, *Methods and Means Utilized in Cuba to Eliminate Illiteracy* (Havana: Editora Pedagogica, 1965), p. 72.

17. Ibid.

18. Ibid.

19. Kozol, *Children of the Revolution*, p. 62.

20. Ibid., p. 70.

21. Ibid., p. 31.

22. Ibid., p. 22.

23. Ibid.

24. Mujica, "Recollections," p. 224.

25. Ibid.

26. Ibid.

27. UNESCO, *Methods and Means*, p. 72.

28. Ibid., p. 73.

29. Paulo Freire, *The Pedagogy of the Oppressed* (New York: Herder and Herder, 1970), p. 175.

30. Kozol, *Children of the Revolution*, p. 18.

31. Ibid.

32. Ibid.

33. UNCTAD, *Health and Educational Technology*, p. 10.

34. Ibid., p. 11.

35. Ibid., p. 15.

36. Ibid.

37. Rolland G. Paulson, *Pre-Conditions for Systems-Wide Educational Reform: Learning from the Cuban Experience* (Chicago: ERIC Document Reproduction Service, ED 128–250, April 1976), p. 4.

38. Ibid., p. 18.

39. Ibid.

40. Ibid.

41. Ibid., p. 19.

42. Ibid., p. 20.

43. Ibid.

44. Karen Wald, *Children of Che: Childcare and Education in Cuba* (Palo Alto, Calif.: Ramparts Press, 1978), p. 163.

45. Douglas Butterworth, *The People of Buena Ventura: Relocation of Slum Dwellers in Post-Revolutionary Cuba* (Urbana: University of Illinois Press, 1980), p. 95.

46. Ibid., p. 141.

47. Jorge I. Dominguez, *Cuba: Order and Revolution* (Cambridge, Mass.: Harvard University Press, 1978), p. 171.

48. American Association of State Colleges and Universities,

Impressions of the Republic of Cuba (Chicago: ERIC Document Reproduction Service, ED 185–895, November 1979), p. 29.

49. Ibid.

50. Center for Cuban Studies, *Cuba Update* 1, no. 6 (January 1981), p. 3.

51. Abel Prieto Morales, "A Conversation with Abel Prieto," *Journal of Reading* 25, no. 3 (December 1981), p. 236.

52. Interview with José R. Fernández, minister of education, Havana, May 14, 1983.

53. Interview with Merida Lopez, researcher, Ministry of Education, Havana, May 9, 1983.

54. Ibid.

55. Center for Cuban Studies, *Cuba Update*, p. 4.

56. Lopez interview, May 1983.

57. Fernández interview, May 1983.

58. Lopez interview, May 1983.

59. Ibid.

60. Ibid.

61. Ministry of Education, *Report of the Republic of Cuba to the 38th International Conference on Public Education* (Havana, 1981), p. 66.

62. Fernández interview, May 1983.

63. Dominguez, *Order and Revolution*, p. 264.

64. Ibid., p. 262.

65. Morales, "A Conversation with Abel Prieto," p. 266.

66. Wald, *Children of Che*, p. 192.

67. Urie Bronfenbrenner, *Two Worlds of Childhood* (New York: Simon & Schuster, 1970), p. 47.

68. Ibid., p. 38.

69. Ibid., p. 47.

70. Wald, *Children of Che*, p. 187.

71. Center for Cuban Studies, *Cuba Update*, p. 1.

72. Ibid., pp. 1–12.

73. UNCTAD, *Health and Educational Technology*, p. 18.

74. Center for Cuban Studies, *Cuba Update*, p. 12.

75. Ibid.

76. Marvin Leiner, "Two Decades of Educational Change in Cuba," *Journal of Reading* 25, no. 3 (December 1981), p. 211.

77. Morales, "A Conversation with Abel Prieto," p. 267.

78. Samuel Bowles, "Cuban Education and the Revolutionary Ideology," *Harvard Educational Review* 41, no. 4 (November 1971), p. 476.

79. Fidel Castro, *Education in Revolution* (Havana: Instituto Cubano Del Libro, 1975), pp. 143–44.

80. Kozol, *Children of the Revolution*, p. 175.

81. Ibid.

82. Interview with Sara Gonzalez, director of International Relations Section of the Ernesto "Che" Guevara Pioneer Palace, Havana, May 12, 1983.

83. Interview with Magaly García Ojeda, director of primary schools, Ministry of Education, Havana, May 10, 1983.

84. Ibid.

85. Cecelia Pollack and Victor Martuza, "Teaching Reading in the Cuban Primary Schools," *Journal of Reading* 25, no. 3 (December 1981), p. 241.

86. Ibid., p. 242.

87. Butterworth, *The People of Buena Ventura*, p. 141.

7
CUBA'S MOST SUCCESSFUL SCHOOLS AND PROGRAMS

Because there are marked differences between urban schools in Cuba and the United States, it would be useful to examine the character of Cuban urban schools. In May 1983, I traveled to Havana to conduct a limited study of Cuban schools. The purpose of the study was to collect recent data on Cuban education, visit schools and observe classroom teaching, and interview key officials in the Ministry of Education concerning urban education in Cuba.

One of the purposes of this chapter is to augment the paucity of firsthand accounts of Cuban education. That dearth has been due primarily to two factors: the boycott of Cuba by the United States shortly after the Revolution (which was lifted in terms of travel by the Carter administration in 1977 and reinstated five years later by the Reagan administration) and the fact that the prevailing scholarship in this country has been done by Cuban exiles who have not been permitted to return for obvious reasons of security. As a result, there are scarcely more than a half-dozen U.S. scholars and journalists who have written firsthand accounts of Cuban education. None has concentrated on urban schools.

Under the terms of restrictions imposed in May 1982 by the Reagan administration, only scholars conducting research and accredited journalists were permitted to travel to Cuba. After securing the promise of funding from my university, Old Dominion, I applied to the Cuban Ministry of Education to conduct a limited study of Cuban urban education. My request was sent to the Cuban Interest Section in Washington, D.C., and forwarded to the ministry. I outlined the scope of my study and related personal background material. In February 1983, the Cuban authorities contacted Jonathan Kozol, the American educator who had written of the Cuban Literacy Campaign, for a reference. I was not personally acquainted with Kozol, but had written him for aid in contacting the proper Cuban authorities. He was kind enough to inform Cuban officials in Washington that he knew and admired my work "on community control in New York City" and concluded that I would be "an excellent observer of the Cuban situation."[1] Kozol's recommendation impressed the Cuban authorities, and they agreed to allow me to conduct my study in Havana in May after my classes at the university were completed.

The Cuban ministry then asked for specific research plans. I forwarded a letter outlining my three goals: I asked to speak to a researcher who would be able to give me data, to visit specific schools, and to interview specific educational officials. In order to obtain a socioeconomic contrast, I requested to visit two primary schools, one in the *solares* or tenement sections of Old Havana, where many poor lived before the Revolution, and one in the Vedado section, formerly an affluent area of the city. In addition, I wanted to observe a junior high school. Unfortunately, both schools (which I had read about in Karen Wald's *Children of Che*), were no longer in operation, but comparable primary schools were included in the itinerary. I also cited specific officials that I wished to interview concerning urban education: the director of primary schools, the deputy minister of education, and the minister of education. All requests were honored by the Cuban ministry. I had limited my investigations to Cuban primary and intermediate schools in Havana, knowing full well that most high schools were boarding schools in the countryside; I felt that visiting these schools would detract from my urban mission. In retrospect, that decision may have been ill-considered, for most newer facilities, for example, were schools-in-the-countryside.

Havana is a city of some 2 million. Its outstanding character is that it is without slums, a fact corroborated by other writers who have visited. In my extensive travels throughout the city, there was no instance of the type of slum that characterizes so much of Latin American countries. On the other hand, Havana has little of the radiance that distinguishes comparable cities in the United States—with their slums and ghettoes. The best hotel, for example, was built prior to the Revolution. Since the Revolution, most hotel construction has been for workers and peasants in the countryside. Cubans acknowledge that one of the problems of the Revolution has been housing. Nonetheless, there are little of the outward signs of poverty in Havana.

Officials at the Ministry of Education contend that there is little concern with urban schooling as a separate issue. Magaly García Ojeda, director of primary education, stated, "There is no special orientation toward urban education but . . . we have a unique study plan to be applied in all schools in the towns, countryside and mountains."[2] As previously described, students at urban schools are not a serious discipline problem, nor do school buildings reflect the graffiti or vandalism so often a result of student hostility in the United States.

The first school visited was the Manuel Valdes Rodriguez Primary School in Vedado, a wealthy neighborhood prior to the Revolution. (It was named after a Cuban teacher.) This school, built in 1949, was rather shopworn and old, desperately needing a coat of paint inside the building. The school also had the dubious distinction of having its auditorium completely gutted as the result of sabotage a few years earlier. The school had an enrollment of some 1,067 children, 39 teachers (one was on loan to Nicaragua), and 119 staff members, including cooks, librarians, dining-hall assistants, and a gardener. The school was a semiboarding school, which meant that students ate lunch there and stayed until early evening when they were brought home by working mothers.[3]

The principal was a young woman in her early thirties, Maria Elena Torrez Arazo. Upon entering her office, a visitor from the United States receives a mild culture shock. Directly behind her desk is a huge picture of Ho Chi Minh, the leader of the Vietnamese revolution. Indeed, in all of the schools and in the offices of educational officials were portraits of current and deceased revolutionary leaders, usually those of the Cuban Revolution. This was the first instance of a picture of a revolutionary leader from another country.

The school was excellent. The rate of attendance was 98.7 percent, the rate of punctuality 99.5 percent, and the promotion rate 96.43 percent. Walking through the dark halls, one could perceive the educational ambience. When there was noise, it was educational noise, the process of learning. It could be compared, slightly, to the atmosphere of an open school in the United States. One mathematics class in the fifth grade was subdued and intent. The teacher appeared slightly intimidated by the visitors (including a representative from the Ministry of Education, Merida Lopez)—who might have made any teacher nervous. The class was comprised of twenty-nine students in a rather bare room with pictures of Fidel Castro and José Martí on display. The teacher employed a question-and-answer method and called on all the children. The class appeared bright and interested, differing little from a good fifth-grade class in the United States—except in the starkness of the classroom in terms of displays. Teachers in the United States are encouraged by their principals to have children contribute to creating elaborate displays to be placed on the walls. There appears to be none of that in Cuban schools.

I also visited a third-grade class having a Spanish lesson. The thirty-one students became so animated that they appeared not to notice the visiting delegation. The teacher engaged the attention of all students, calling on a representative sample, and the level of student interest was so high as to make this class a rather exceptional one by any standards. The class was racially integrated, with a good number of black Cuban children represented. The room had its by now obligatory picture of a revolutionary hero, in this case, "Che" Guevara.

Between classes, a delegation of leaders from the Pioneers was permitted to join an informal discussion. In primary schools, there are two sets of Pioneers. One group, from grades one through four, is called *Moncadistas* (after the attack on Moncada by the Revolutionary leaders). The *Moncadistas* wear red pants or skirts with a white blouse but sport a blue bandanna. The older students, grades five through six, have red bandannas. (That red bandanna is also a mark of intermediate and secondary schools, but with different colored pants and skirts.) The older group is part of the José Martí Brigade of Pioneers, named after the hero of the war for independence from Spain.

The Pioneer delegation was comprised completely of girls in the sixth grade. The only male member of the Pioneer leadership was in charge of sports. This pattern of girls dominating Pioneer leadership seems to hold true for primary and intermediate school and corresponds to the U.S. pattern of girls maturing earlier than boys. The Pioneer delegation outlined the task of the interest circles, described their personal interest circles, and outlined their main responsibilities, which include monitoring student attendance, discipline, and promotion rates. Moreover, the Pioneers are involved in what is described as "socially useful work." This entails small jobs around the school such as weeding the garden, picking up papers, collecting garbage, taking care of the bulletin board, and reporting to the carpenter work that requires repairs.

The delegation seemed to be a rather serious group of students. The school principal boasted of a 100 percent enrollment in the Pioneers, and that "none had any religious beliefs."[4] The principal was also proud of other features of her school. For example, a dentist was assigned to it, and there was a small dispensary. She pointed out that teachers receive what would be called in the United States "in-service" training. They receive additional training once a month, from 8:00 A.M. to 1:00 P.M., on Saturdays, to update course content.

Another primary school visited was in the Plaza de la Revolución section of Havana, in what can best be described as a middle-class area. The school, Ejercito Rebelde ("Rebel Army"), is housed in a relatively new building built nine years ago. It is also a semiboarding school with eight-hundred students. The principal, Nilda Jimenez, was a young black woman in her early thirties who appeared quite confident and competent. Again, the essential educational statistics of the students were quite positive: Attendance was 98.5 percent, and promotion rates were 96.6 percent for the previous year.[5] As in the first primary school, there were no traces of graffiti or vandalism on buildings.

A tour of classes that were not in session revealed the paucity of resources that hampers Cuban education. There were few of the apparatuses needed in the laboratory, and a comparison with a United States lab would place these classrooms in a poor light. The same was true of school workshops. On the other hand, the library would fare favorably with U.S. elementary school libraries.

The principal outlined the tasks of the School Council. In addition to monitoring attendance, discipline, and promotion rates, the council has other less serious duties. It arranges for school parties on such days as "Mothers' Day," "Education Day," the end-of-school party, and similar functions. As has been mentioned, each class has a parental delegate to the School Council, and the council president is a parent. There are four parent assemblies scheduled during the year with extra sessions planned as the occasion warrants. Parents are encouraged to become volunteers in the school as time permits. The principal finds that the work of the School Council is important to the school's functioning.

The intermediate school I visited, José Antonio Echeverría Intermediate School, was named after the Revolutionary hero who was a student leader at the University of Havana and killed by Battista. This school, housed in an old office building in the center of Old Havana, occupied two floors reached by·an elevator, and the classrooms (except for the science classrooms) were small. The school encompasses the seventh, eighth, and ninth grades and had an enrollment of 1,599 students, somewhat large for its cramped situation. The principal, Allan Gutierrez, was a chain-smoking, intense young man in his early thirties. A picture of Lenin was displayed prominently in his office.

The school had been the recipient of numerous awards from the province and the Ministry of Education. These awards were kept in a room adjacent to the principal's office. He was proud of the student attendance rate of 98 percent, the punctuality rate of 98 percent, and the promotion rate of 94.5 percent for the current year. There were a significant number of black students at this school. Again, the Pioneer leadership that I talked to consisted almost wholly of girls.

Echeverria School had significantly more murals on the hallway walls than other schools visited. Created by both students and faculty, they depicted martyrs and heroes of Latin America. Parents volunteered money for some of the murals. The School Council representative from the Communist party, a young black woman, was in charge of the "ideological and political" work with students, which includes the painting of political murals.

The students travel to the countryside for forty-five days each year to work and study. This stint is timed with those of other schools to assure continuity in the harvest. The students live in the countryside and either study in the morning and work in the afternoon or the reverse. Light work is involved, and not the strenuous work of cutting sugarcane.

Once again, the school principal, teachers, and students affirmed that discipline was not a major problem in Cuban schools. The principal maintained that the teachers could handle whatever small discipline problem arose. Gutierrez emphasized that Cuban students spend considerable amounts of time learning manners, use and care of the uniform, and the like.[6] Indeed, in all the schools visited, the students were neat, and their uniforms appeared well-cared-for.

At this stage, students begin to learn either Russian or English. In their literature courses they study Spanish, Caribbean, and Cuban literature, successively each year. Students in the literary interest circle read Jack London and Ernest Hemingway, along with Chekhov, Marx, and Nicholas Guillen, among others. There was more reading of international authors in the preuniversity high schools.

One classroom visited was a seventh-grade biology class situated in a spacious room where the teacher employed audiovisual aids. However, the wall was dark and needed a lighter coat of paint to make maximum use of the projector. This was a lively class, and the students responded to the teacher's question-and-answer methodology. It was in this class that the first of two noteworthy incidents occurred. The teacher called several times on a young man who was extremely bright.

The boy was not wearing a red bandanna, the symbol of membership in the Pioneers. The president of the Pioneers informed me during the course of the lesson that the student was a member of the Jehovah's Witnesses and the son of devout parents. She asserted that the Pioneer leaders had sought to have the young Witness join their ranks, but to no avail. The incident appeared to be wholly unstaged, and the absence of discrimination by the teacher against one of a minority viewpoint was notable. The teacher called on this student many times, apparently because he was intelligent.

Another incident occurred that touched me. In a staged welcome to the school, a number of Pioneers were grouped in a circle with myself at the head. A young black girl approached me, removed her red bandanna, placed it around my neck, and kissed me on both cheeks. This sincerity and goodwill embarrassed me, as I recalled that I was, perhaps, misrepresenting myself since I did not fully share her philosophy.

One of the most satisfying visits in my tour was to a day care center, Grandes Alamedas, located in the Plaza de la Revolución section of the city. The facilities were relatively new, bright, and well kept, and the children happy and relaxed. The day care center has a capacity of 240 with a ratio of one supervisor-educator for every 8 children. Their ages ranged from forty-five days to six years, with the children divided by age into eight groups. The center was open from 6 A.M. to 7 P.M., when mothers returning from work could bring their children home. The center maintained a doctor (in this case, a Soviet woman who had married a Cuban), and she kept regular and comprehensive records; a dentist was also available to the center.

The center's main goal was play. However, educational activities were interwoven in the fabric of life there, and social development was emphasized. Music, art, and math were also part of the program. One lesson observed for three-year-olds had as the main objective learning how to grasp a coffeepot. There were twelve children in this group, and the instructor had them cut and paste a drawing of a coffeepot. The children were so intent on their lesson and activity that they paid scarce attention to the visitors.

The day care center was substantially integrated. Many black children played with the white children amiably and cooperatively. This was the case also with a class of five-year-olds involved in free dance. This group, which included a child from the United States whose parents were conducting research in Cuba, engaged in a dance led by their instructor.

The day care center had some of the characteristics of the regular school. One room contained a patriotic corner where children brought cutouts of revolutionary heroes. The older children maintained a garden. The center also had a Parents' Council with regular assemblies: One of its aims was to interest parents in performing voluntary work. And, as the personnel delighted in stating, this center was free of charge, and all materials and food were also without cost to the families. There are now approximately one-hundred-thousand children in day care centers. The ratio of children to supervisors and the necessity for intensive medical care contribute to the high cost of most.

The last facility I should like to discuss is the José Martí City of Pioneers. This installation, located on the ocean ten miles from Havana, combines study and recreation for fifteen days for Pioneers selected from the schools with the highest promotion rates. José Martí City houses ten thousand Pioneers at one time in 526 beach houses (formerly owned by affluent Cubans prior to the Revolution) and 5 dormitories. It is the largest such facility in the world, surpassing those built in the Soviet Union.

The facility opened in 1975 as a small camp and was enlarged and reopened as a city in 1978. Besides beaches, there is a lake that accommodates boating, a small park with an outdoor movie screen and amphitheater, an aviary, suspension cable cars, a hospital for the Pioneers, and specialized hospitals for diabetics and asthmatics. (The Revolutionary leader Ernesto "Che" Guevara suffered from asthma and was sent to this ocean place to recuperate long before it became a student recreational center.) Indeed, three separate bungalows are set aside to honor Cuban heroes: one for Guevara, where he lived; one for Celia Sanchez, a Revolutionary hero who died a few years ago; and one for José Martí. These are manned by Pioneers and display photographs and memorabilia of the lives of the honored persons.

The students alternate study and play and are given a diploma when they leave. A Pioneers Council oversees group behavior. The Pioneers are divided into five camps of approximately two thousand each. Not all students come to the City of Pioneers. Students who are not Pioneers because of religious belief may not wish to attend, although they, also, are welcome. Parents come and visit their children on Sundays. The students often bring roller skates and kites from home for recreation.

Camp and school officials maintain that Pioneers perform better academically in this setting than in regular classrooms. Two nights a week are set aside for study in addition to the regular homework hours. Officials maintain that the new atmosphere spurs motivation. Incidentally, teachers from the schools join the Pioneers in this outing.

During the summer vacation months, the José Martí City hosts Pioneer delegations from socialist and some nonsocialist countries. Eighty to ninety Pioneers from the Antonio Maceo brigade in the United States come for a month in the summer. Leaders of the Revolution, especially Fidel Castro, are frequent visitors to José Martí City. Each province, however, has it own City of Pioneers.

I met with the minister of education, José R. Fernández, at the end of my stay. The meeting was scheduled for an odd hour, six P.M. on a Saturday, but it proved extremely fruitful. Fernández is a dynamic, imposing figure who spent some time at Fort Sill, Oklahoma, in the 1950s. A leader of the Revolution, he was jailed by Battista. He distinguished himself as Premier Castro's chief troop commander in what we in this country call the Bay of Pigs invasion. His initial remarks concerned the need for a political rapprochement between Cuba and the United States, and he then proceeded to answer questions concerning educational conditions in Cuba. His manner was not at all defensive, but candid and helpful.

Officials at the Ministry of Education are quite frank about the problems they perceive to continue to plague the Cuban educational system. Fernández divided these problems into two categories: material and human. Material problems, he conceded, involve the need to repair schools and keep them in good condition. My visits to Cuban urban schools indicated that some city schools are old and need restoration and coats of paint. In addition, the minister noted the lack of financial resources, at present, to buy equipment such as school supplies. Again, in visiting biology and chemistry classrooms, the paucity of equipment compared to that of a well-stocked United States classroom was painfully obvious to me. Finally, the minister noted the shortage of paper for the publication of books.

The human problems, he stated, were mainly those of improving quality. Such improvement entails raising the level of teacher preparation and involving parents in the educational process to improve study habits of students. He would like to see students study a few more hours per week. Some parents, he said, complain that they can not handle their children, especially teenagers. But a closer relationship between parents and school would engender more scholarly behavior among students.[7]

In summary, the general impression that one receives is of an increasingly effective school system. Classroom teaching appears to be somewhat similar in style to that in the United States. However, Cuban teachers do not have the university preparation possessed by teachers in the United States. As for facilities and equipment, this is one area where Cuban schools need additional resources. Students seem more serious and disciplined than their urban U.S. counterparts.

One final impression concerning hostility to U.S. citizens must be recorded. During my stay in Cuba, I was welcomed warmly. There was no animosity from students, education personnel, or Cuban citizens. Nonetheless, the legacy of American foreign policy is deeply felt. For example, the last exhibit at the Museum of the City, which houses artifacts concerning Cuba's history until the Revolution, is the remnant of a huge black eagle presented by the United States.

This eagle, which overlooked the ocean in Havana, was broken by angry Cubans after the Bay of Pigs invasion. Next to this symbol of political dominance is a symbol of economic dominance; a wooden carton with empty Coca-Cola bottles. Cuba no longer is under the influence of the United States.

Notes

1. Letter from Jonathan Kozol to Maurice R. Berube, February 25, 1983.
2. Interview with Magaly García Ojeda, director of primary schools, Ministry of Education, Havana, May 10, 1983.
3. Interview with Maria Elena Torrez Arazo, principal, Manuel Valdes Rodriguez Primary School, Havana, May 10, 1983.
4. Ibid.
5. Interview with Nilda Jimenez, principal, Ejercito Rebelde Primary School, May 11, 1983.
6. Interview with Allan Gutierrez, principal, José Antonio Echeverría Intermediate School, Havana, May 12, 1983.
7. Interview with José R. Fernández, minister of education, Havana, May 14, 1983.

PART THREE: Synthesis

8
IMPLICATIONS AND RECOMMENDATIONS

We have discovered that in the United States, some low income groups achieved respectably in schools in the past and that some low income students perform well in urban schools at present. In Cuba, the 1961 Literacy Campaign brought poor Cubans up to a literate level, and Cuban schools are effective at the elementary school level.

There is still much to learn, however, about the relationship of poverty to education, and one must maintain perspective in discussing the educational systems of these two distinctly political opposites. First, there is the question of size. With approximately 9 million citizens, Cuba has but a fraction of the U.S. population of some 234 million. Educationally, Cuba would be comparable in size to the New York City school district. Second, the Cuban people and their culture are much more homogeneous than the polyglot blend of nationalities and subcultures in the United States. Third, and most important, Cuba is still an economically underdeveloped nation compared with the highly developed United States. As Lester Thurow points out in *The Zero Sum Society*, U.S. prosperity is due as much to the fact that we inherited a nation tremendously rich in resources as it is to our ingenuity.[1] Fourth, the absence of poverty in Cuban cities compares favorably with the condition of American cities. In that respect, the socialistic system has as its chief aim the elimination of poverty.

Perhaps the greatest caution must concern a comparison of the economic base of the Cuban and American school systems. Cuba is at best a developing country, and its educators are painfully aware of shortages in supplies. Whereas Cuban educators talk about the need for more paper for textbooks, U.S. educators are considering placing computers in classrooms. In this context, it would be fairer to compare the Cuban educational system with those of other Latin American countries. In that light, Cuba is singular in its commitment to and development of education.

Most important, in a comparative study, there is a question of quality. What we have been considering in this investigation is a minimum educational level—that is, a basic level of education for the poor and not necessarily enriched or higher levels of quality. The focus is on the average and not the highest percentile; on a minimally educated person, not on the development of an Einstein (although such a product is much desired). In that respect, nations can provide a standard for effectiveness.

Implications of the U.S. Experience

One must also maintain perspective in discussing education in the United States. For example, the United States has more full-time students in the fifteen-to-nineteen group (75 percent) than, for example, France and Germany (51 percent).[2] Moreover, 85 percent of American white high school students graduate, and slightly less than half of the college age population is in institutions of higher learning; this is the largest proportion in the world by far. One could read these figures with satisfaction.

On the other hand, the large number of poor in the cities fare badly in the schools. In New York City, nearly 1 million of the 8 million population are welfare poor, and double that number could be considered near poor. The dropout rate in New York City high schools is 45 percent.[3] Forty-nine percent of elementary and junior high school students in New York City are more than one year behind in reading levels.[4]. This constitutes a two-track system of education; one for the urban poor, where failure is the norm, and one for the suburban middle class and affluent, where achievement is routine.

It has been shown, both in the past and the present, that some low income students learn adequately and that some schools are effective in educating an urban poor. These students and these schools, unfortunately, are still the exception rather than the rule. Nonetheless, the research is impressive attesting to the success of some. The task is to translate the techniques that make the few succeed into educational strategies that will benefit the many.

Implications of the Cuban Experience

We are interested in Cuban schools mainly because of the lessons that can be derived. But it must be remembered that our investigations into Cuban education have been far from exhaustive. The political context does not permit such a venture (U.S. cold war policies inhibit such scholarship), nor am I the proper researcher to provide a definitive study of Cuban education (my interest for the past twenty-five years has been in American schools). Nonetheless, the success of the Cuban Revolution in educating the poor to literacy and providing effective education has much to recommend it.

Although the research is not as sophisticated and strong as that found in the United States, an examination of the Cuban educational experience since the Revolution offers some tentative implications. First, the Cuban educational system appears to be successful in the Literacy Campaign, at the elementary level, and, increasingly, at the intermediate level. Variables that coincide with U.S. research findings are high teacher expectations and significant parental involvement. In addition, the lessening of poverty could be seen to have some beneficial effect. Other educational reforms, structural in content, do not correspond to U.S. scholarship but could be incentives for American educators to follow. One practice, in particular, that might have positive effects would be to have the same teacher for the first four years.

Recommendations

The success of the few effective schools in the United States and the success in Cuba suggests four broad recommendations. These four and the rationale that accompanies them are presented in ascending order of difficulty of achievement in the United States, given the educational politics of the land. They are: 1. create effective school models and pursue more research; 2. create national urban student and parental organizations as is done in Cuba; 3. create a national system of education that would provide uniform leadership; and 4. eliminate poverty.

1. Create Effective School Models

The effective schools movement has shown that the poor can be sufficiently educated if the proper circumstances exist. These variables include academic leadership from principals, high expectations from teachers, rigorous academic work, and significant parental innvolvement. Surely, these are realizable goals in time.

Nevertheless, one must be cautious concerning the claims of some in the effective schools movement. Some critics maintain that the movement is more "a rhetoric of reform" than a "scientific model."[5] In the same vein, some educators despair that "no one knows how to create effective schools" because of the vague implications of the research.[6] Still, the findings of some researchers are cause for hope for urban schools.

What are we to conclude of this scholarship of the past few years? First, it has opened up debate and new areas of knowledge previously closed and unexamined. Second, it has seriously questioned the thrust of American educational policy for the past century. It is a tragedy that our system of education is not a thought-out, smoothly working, organized operation. The fact that educational power resides with the states—a nearly anachronistic governmental body—and that educators adhere to the ineffective rubric of local control makes for an educational system and policy that at best work at cross-purposes and at worst serve to benefit those who are already rich in resources and advantages.

Two aims in urban education must be pursued simultaneously. First, models of effective schools should continue to be implemented in urban school districts. Moreover, further research should be encouraged, especially more intensive longitudinal studies to seek and find the answers to effective education of low-income students, thereby contributing to better effective schools models.

2. Create National Urban Student and Parental Organizations

Student motivation can be increased through the creation of national urban student and parental organizations that would have real roles in running the schools along with the administration and teacher unions. Teacher unions now control much of the power of urban schooling (formally through their bargaining power concerning the 75–80 percent of school budgets that is allocated to salaries, and informally through the suggestion of educational programs and the setting of teacher and academic standards).

These student organizations need not have the paramilitary aspect of the Pioneers (either in Cuba or the Soviet Union), but they could be educational organizations, somewhat like the Pioneers, concentrating on tasks such as promotion rates, discipline, and care of property. They could have other activities as well. Yet they should not be treated with paternalism by school administrators but should be regarded as partners.

This holds true for parental organizations as well. Not only should parents have a real voice in determining school policy through elected school boards with significant power, but a national organization of urban parents should seek to become another partner in the running of the schools. Their tasks would be primarily educational also. They would seek to increase promotion and discipline.

3. Create a National Educational System

Education in the United States is more of a "happening" than an orderly, well-thought-out system, primarily because the founding fathers neglected the importance of education.

They simply did not provide for it in the Constitution. As a result, education—through default—has become the province of the states, since all powers not specifically mentioned in the Constitution and attributed to the federal government have been interpreted as the domain of the states. Unfortunately, such an arrangement has resulted in an uneven and unequal public education system in this country.

Consider the matter of financial resources. Since most states have placed the financial burden on localities, inequity has resulted. Localities base school finance mostly on property taxes, and property-rich school districts, such as in wealthy suburbs of large cities, can raise more for schools than can poor rural counties. That is an unequal distribution within states. And the amount of educational monies raised by a poor state like Mississippi differs considerably from that of a wealthy state like California. The end result is an inequitable financial public school system whose quality varies from school district to school district and from state to state.

Within the past generation, back-door efforts have been made to strengthen national control over public education. The federal government has attempted to provide direction on a categorical—that is, a needs or issue—basis. Needless to say, these efforts are not in the spirit of the Constitution but seek an ad hoc arrangement with the schools. Although most such efforts, especially in the last generation, have had some beneficial effect, we still lack a central national focus on *all* of public education.

What is needed is a national commitment to education. The United States should have a national educational institution supervising the conduct of public schooling in the states and localities. That institution must be so constructed as to sensitively incorporate some measure of the tradition of local control. One model may be the old poverty program in President Lyndon Johnson's war on poverty in the 1960s. As originally conceived, the Office of Economic Opportunity set national policy, with input and implementation at the local level. That allowed for local initiative. The task is to design a national commitment in order to raise the quality of education to an acceptable national level while creating a role for localities, so as to provide variety.

One false start in the direction of such a national initiative is the work of a body of educators, known as *The Paideia Proposal*.[7] They include the philosopher Mortimer Adler; the former provost of Columbia University, Jacques Barzun; and the head of Chicago schools, Ruth B. Love. Working under a grant from the MacArthur Foundation, this group of educators considered the most urgent need in reforming public-school education. With an astonishing misreading of the state of public education in the United States, they concluded that what was required to improve schooling was a national academic curriculum for all. Quoting Robert Maynard Hutchins, they proclaimed a rather elitist standard: "The best education for the best," he said, "is the best education for all." The Paideia group concluded, "We should have a one-track system of schooling, not a system with two or more tracks, only one of which goes straight ahead while the others shunt the young off onto sidetracks not headed toward the goals our society opens to all.[8]

The Paideia Proposal would do away with vocational education. It would offer a uniform program of language, literature, and the fine arts, mathematics and natural science, history and geography, and social studies. The proposal was endorsed by the most educationally conservative in the nation. Albert Shanker, for example, president of the American Federation of Teachers, was overwhelming in his praise in a book-jacket endorsement. He predicted that it would "dominate education discussion for the next decade." Moreover, "it goes overboard in the right direction."[9]

What is neglected, of course, is that students develop learning proclivities and abilities at different times in their lives, and respond to different approaches. A method such as Montessori, which works well with one child, might not be as worthwhile with another. The direction of recent research points toward different teaching and learning styles and the need for variety in American education through alternatives in an otherwise monochromatic public education system. The Paideia Proposal is a misguided attempt to retreat to a mythical past and runs counter to the educational advances made in the United States—few though they have been—in the past generation.

4. Eliminate Poverty

Educators place little stress on the politics of education, too often feeling that education and politics should be separated. Yet in truth, education is dependent on the political process. State legislatures determine the structure, financial arrangements, and standards of education. Some educators are beginning to realize this. The teachers' union in New York City, for example, employs three full-time staff members year round to lobby in the state legislature for laws favorable to teachers and the union. The union also makes sizeable financial contributions to legislative candidates, and its members volunteer as campaign workers. This political acumen has paid dividends in support for union-sponsored educational legislation. Nevertheless, this political awareness is still the exception rather than the rule among teachers and administrators. One hears too frequently of educational reformers recommending alliances of school people with business or, say, the general public without reference to the need for political pressure. Some high-minded educational reformers offer their suggestions to the public without the slightest sense of the politics of education and the need to translate those ideas into political pressure.

Most important, education does not take place in a vacuum. It is crucially linked to the political, social, and economic aspects of a society. Too often education has been isolated and considered apart from the influence of larger forces in the society. Unfortunately, the proponents of effective schools have neglected the political, social, and economic matrix. Some of these proponents, it is true, are concerned mainly with the scholarly aspect of their investigations. Others argue strongly for much needed educational reform—but without political, social, and economic consideration.

As a result, one of the problems in fashioning educational policy is that it is determined apart from other societal forces. Not only is the politics of education neglected, but the very matrix of education is ignored. The Revisionist educational historians were able to strongly underline this point. They perceived education in its larger political, economic, and social context. In *Schooling in a Capitalist America*, Samuel Bowles and Herbert Gintis try to link economics with education. They portray a public school system that is the handmaiden of a capitalistic economic system.[10] Although their analysis makes too close a connection between the public schools and the capitalist economy, these authors were on the right track. The educational system is too poorly planned, structurally decentralized, and inefficient to make for a strong alliance with the needs of businesses, as Bowles and Gintis suggest. Nevertheless, an economic function of the public schools does exist.

Likewise the political matrix of education is ignored. Curricula regulations and philosophies of education are geared mostly for the preservation of the status quo. Frederick Wiseman's brilliant film *High School* is an incriminating portrait of teachers and administrators in a middle-class Philadelphia school. The staff at this school blindly and uncritically indoctrinates the goals of the prevailing national administration in a raging war in Vietnam. There is no mention by these school people of the deep controversy over the issue of Vietnam. Frances Fitzgerald has shown in her work the historical neglect of controversial issues in American textbooks.[11] The result is not the ends of education—critical thinking—but an indoctrination of the merits of a certain philosophy in America. Such a practice in a socialist state is readily condemned in the United States.

That is to say, the politics of a nation also come to bear on the shape and content of education. And the ends of national purpose have influence on what is taught in the fourth grade and how it is taught. That is as it should be. There are national educational needs, such as the grooming of scientists and technicians to forward national defense and the growth of a developed economy. No one is quarreling with that function of education. But a blind obeisance by school people to whatever national policy is conducted is far from desirable. A national policy that neglects the poor, blacks, women, and other minorities does not have the necessary compassion nor the ideal of social justice.

There are large political questions to be answered. Can the

United States effectively educate a majority of its urban poor within the constraints of its political and economic system? That question has been largely ignored by the effective schools movement. Proponents assume that effective education is possible on a large scale without substantially altering the conditions of the urban poor. Other educators are not so sure. Some, like the Revisionists Samuel Bowles and Herbert Gintis, conclude that some form of American socialism is required *before* the schools can effectively perform their mandated functions.[12] The effective schools movement could profit from calling for programs to eliminate poverty.

And can that task be accomplished without radically restructuring the society? Certainly, not as our system of government and economics has been construed in the past. The liberal economist Lester Thurow shows in *The Zero Sum Society* that unemployment and poverty are staples of our system except in times of war. Since the private sector has historically proven itself incapable of providing full employment, he recommends that the public sector—government—become the employer of last resort.[13]

On the other hand, it must also be noted that many educational commentators argue for a consideration of societal factors *exclusive* of educational reform. This was especially true in the decade of school reform in the 1960s, when maintainers of the status quo criticized educational reformers for neglecting the deleterious effects of urban poverty in the nation. It was argued that schools should not be forced to bear the entire brunt of society's ills alone. First, employment, housing, and health care should be improved. That line of reasoning also is defective. It permits political leaders and the public to tolerate bad conditions until the long awaited social revolution takes place. (It must be mentioned that these commentators rarely took up the revolutionary challenge in activist fashion for the desired changes they sought.)

Educational change is truly dependent on, social change. However, one must not put off the one until the other is achieved. Reformers should seek educational change while also seeking broader social change. It is unlikely that school reforms can achieve lasting performance without broader social change.

Most urban schools fail. A small minority are successful, but we do not know whether their recipe for success can be applied to the rest of urban schools. It is also crucial to link efforts to eliminate poverty so as to make urban school reform more plausible. The bulk of the historical evidence suggests that the eradication of poverty in this nation would facilitate schooling of the poor. Because of the ideological bent of the nation and its leaders, it remains to be seen whether this capitalistic economic system can eliminate poverty. Nevertheless, educational reform needs social reform to accompany it. It would make the job of teachers of the poor easier, and it would considerably ease the stress of poor families and enhance student motivation.

The Politics of Educational Reform

We lack a national will to reform the schools. Neither parents nor school officials are interested in deep-seated structural change. This is attested to in national polls of parents, school officials, and teachers concerning perceptions of how the schools are run and the problems to be faced. Gallup polls in recent years have consistently shown that the American public appears satisfied with public schools and gives teachers passing marks.[14] Moreover, it perceives the important school issues to be lack of discipline, use of drugs, and poor standards.[15] The only glimmer of dissatisfaction with the schools comes from citizens living in large cities of over 1 million with substantial urban poverty.

The lack of deep dissatisfaction with public school performance is even more pronounced with school officials. In 1981 school board presidents, superintendents, and elementary and secondary principals were polled following Gallup poll survey questions for the American public. These officials ranked school finance, declining enrollments, and government interference as the major problems facing U.S. public schools.[16] Racial integration was ranked last of eighteen common school problems, paralleling the Gallup poll on public attitudes.[17] Nowhere in either poll was student performance ranked as a major issue. However, in another part of the official school poll, these educators perceived traditional positive influences on school quality. These were teacher interest in students, good parent-teacher relations, and high student aspirations.[18] The last variable emphasizes how school officials place responsibility for achievement mainly upon students rather than upon school resources, echoing the Coleman-Jencks thesis.

Teacher surveys on the chief concerns are even more disappointing. Eight studies conducted by Donald Cruikshank and colleagues over the past fifteen years indicate that teachers are more interested in their own well-being and ease of doing their jobs than in student success. In a list of five major teacher-school issues, teachers ranked as their first concern whether they enjoyed good relationships with other teachers and students. Second was maintaining classroom discipline, and third was obtaining parental support for their efforts.[19] Student achievement was ranked fourth.

These studies indicate that the American public—including school personnel—has little concept of how public schools do their job. Student achievement is either ignored or given low priority. These perceptions are partly due to the lack of solid information on how well schools are doing nationally. Without national standards or national assessment, the picture of public schools that emerges is insufficiently clear to enable us to appraise educational performance. In this respect, one understands why school officials have strenuously opposed national assessments of school performance.

In order for urban school reform to become a reality, there needs to be a political and social movement—a constituency —to seek that reform. It must be composed of urban school parents, civil rights groups, labor organizations, and the citizenry at large. Unfortunately, history has shown that teachers' unions may not deem educational reform to be in the members' best interests. That would be a shortsighted view, since any recipe that succeeds in improving the educational level of failing students would in the long run benefit teachers and their organizations. But matters of power and control can often have mystic effects when people are considering outcomes.

The prime need in this nation is for educational reform that is substantial and deep-seated. First, we must again have hope that educating an urban poor, in significant numbers, is possible. That requires dispatching the myth that the poor are uneducable.

Notes

1. Lester Thurow, *The Zero Sum Society* (New York: Basic Books, 1980).
2. Harold L. Hodgkinson, "What's Still Right with Education," *Phi Delta Kappan* 64, no. 4 (December 1982), p. 233.
3. *New York Times*, March 31, 1983, p. 10.
4. Ibid., April 10, 1983, p. 44.
5. John H. Ralph and James Fennessey, "Science or Reform: Some Questions About the Effective Schools Model," *Phi Delta Kappan* 64, no. 10 (June 1983), p. 693.
6. Larry Cuban, "Effective Schools: A Friendly but Cautionary Note," *Phi Delta Kappan* 64, no. 10 (June 1983), p. 695.
7. Mortimer J. Adler, *The Paideia Proposal* (New York: Macmillan, 1982), p. 6.
8. Ibid., p. 5.
9. Albert Shanker, ibid., book jacket.
10. Samuel Bowles and Herbert Gintis, *Schooling in a Capitalist Society* (New York: Basic Books, 1976).
11. Frances Fitzgerald, *America Revised* (Boston: Little, Brown, 1979).
12. Bowles and Gintis, *Schooling in a Capitalist Society*.
13. Thurow, *The Zero Sum Society*, p. 204.
14. George Gallup, "The 13th Annual Gallup Poll of the Public's Attitudes Toward the Public Schools," *Phi Delta Kappan* 63, no. 1 (September 1981), pp. 35–36.
15. Ibid., p. 34.
16. Jerry Duea, "School Officials and the Public Hold Disparate Views on Education," *Phi Delta Kappan* 63, no. 7 (March 1982), p. 477.
17. Ibid.
18. Ibid., p. 478.
19. Donald R. Cruickshank, "Five Areas of Teacher Concern," *Phi Delta Kappan* 63, no. 7 (March 1982), p. 460.

BIBLIOGRAPHY

Books

Adler, Mortimer. *The Paideia Proposal*. New York: Macmillan, 1982.

Ashline, Nelson F. et al. *Education, Inequality, and National Policy*. Lexington, Mass.: D. C. Heath, 1976.

Banfield, Edward. *The Unheavenly City*. Boston: Little, Brown, 1970.

Benjamin, Robert. *Making Schools Work*. New York: Continuum, 1981.

Blau, Peter M., and Duncan, Otis Dudley. *The American Occupational Structure*. New York: John Wiley and Sons, 1967.

Bloom, Benjamin. *Stability and Change in Human Characteristics*. New York: John Wiley and Sons, 1964.

Blumberg, Arthur, and Greenfield, William. *The Effective Principal*. Boston: Allyn and Bacon, 1980.

Bronfenbrenner, Urie. *Two Worlds of Childhood*. New York: Simon & Schuster, 1970.

Brookover, Wilbur et al. *School Social Systems and Student Achievement*. New York: Praeger, 1979.

Brown, Claude. *Manchild in the Promised Land*. New York: Macmillan, 1965.

Bruner, Jerome. *The Process of Education*. New York: Vintage Books, 1960.

Butterworth, Douglas. *The People of Buena Ventura: Relocation of Slum Dwellers in Post-Revolutionary Cuba*. Urbana, Ill.: University of Illinois Press, 1980.

Castro, Fidel. *Education in Revolution*. Havana: Instituto Cubano Del Libro, 1975.

Comer, James. *School Power.* New York: The Free Press, 1980.

Dominguez, Jorge I. *Cuba: Order and Revolution.* Cambridge, Mass.: Harvard University Press, 1978.

Fitzgerald, Frances. *America Revised.* Boston: Little, Brown, 1979.

Freire, Paulo. *The Pedagogy of the Oppressed.* New York: Herder and Herder, 1970.

Garbarino, James, and Asp, C. Elliot. *Successful Schools and Competent Students.* Lexington, Mass.: Lexington Books, 1981.

Gittell, Marilyn, with Maurice R. Berube et al. *Local Control in Education.* New York: Praeger, 1972.

Goodlad, John. *A Place Called School.* New York: McGraw-Hill, 1983.

Gorelick, Sherry. *City College and the Jewish Poor.* New Brunswick, N.J.: Rutgers University Press, 1981.

Greeley, Andrew M. *Catholic High Schools and Minority Students.* New Brunswick, N.J.: Transaction Books, 1982.

Greeley, Andrew M., and Rossi, Peter. *The Education of Catholic Americans.* Chicago: Aldine, 1966.

Greer, Colin. *The Great School Legend.* New York: Basic Books, 1972.

Gregory, Dick, with Lipsyte, Robert. *Nigger.* New York: E. P. Dutton, 1964.

Hentoff, Nat. *Does Anybody Give a Damn?* New York: Random House, 1976.

————. *Our Children Are Dying.* New York: Viking Press, 1966.

Howe, Irving, with Libo, Kenneth. *World of Our Fathers.* New York: Simon & Schuster, 1976.

Hyman, Herbert et al. *The Enduring Effects of Education.* Chicago: University of Chicago Press, 1975.

Jencks, Christopher et al. *Inequality.* New York: Basic Books, 1972.

————. *Who Gets Ahead?* New York: Basic Books, 1979.

Katz, Michael. *Class, Bureaucracy and Schools.* New York: Praeger, 1972.

Kazin, Alfred. *A Walker in the City.* New York: Harcourt, Brace, 1951.

Kozol, Jonathan. *Children of the Revolution: A Yankee Teacher in the Cuban Schools.* New York: Delacorte Press, 1978.

————. *Death at an Early Age: The Destruction of the Hearts and Minds of Negro Children in the Boston Public Schools.* Boston: Houghton Mifflin, 1967.

Leiner, Marvin, with Ubell, Robert. *Children Are the Revolution: Day Care in Cuba.* New York: Viking Press, 1974.

Levine, Donald, and Bane, Mary Jo, eds. *The 'Inequality' Controversy.* New York: Basic Books, 1975.

Lewis, Oscar. *La Vida.* New York: Random House, 1966.

Lewis, Oscar et al. *Neighbors: Living the Revolution.* Urbana, Ill.: University of Illinois Press, 1978.

Lezotte, Lawrence W. et al. *School Learning Climate and Student Achievement.* Tallahassee, Fla.: Florida State University, 1980.

Lieberson, Stanley. *A Piece of the Pie.* Berkeley Calif.: University of California Press, 1980.

Liebow, Eliot. *Tally's Corner.* Boston: Little, Brown, 1967.

Lightfoot, Sara. *Worlds Apart: Relationships Between Families and Schools.* New York: Basic Books, 1978.

Mayer, Martin. *The Teachers Strike.* New York: Harper & Row, 1969.

Mosteller, Frederick, and Moynihan, Daniel P., eds. *On Equality of Educational Opportunity.* New York: Random House, 1972.

Myrdal, Gunnar et al. *An American Dilemma.* New York: Harper & Row, 1962.

Phi Delta Kappa. *Why Do Some Urban Schools Succeed?* Bloomington, Ind.: Phi Delta Kappa, 1980.

Podhoretz, Norman. *Making It.* New York: Random House, 1967.

Ravitch, Diane. *The Great School Wars.* New York: Basic Books, 1974.

————. *The Revisionists Revised.* New York: Basic Books, 1978.

Ravitch, Diane, and Goodenow, Ronald K., eds. *Educating an Urban People: The New York Experience.* New York: Teachers College Press, 1981.

Rodriguez, Richard. *Hunger of Memory: The Education of Richard Rodriguez.* New York: Bantam Books, 1983.

Rosenthal, Robert, and Jacobson, Lenore. *Pygmalion in the Classroom.* New York: Holt, Rinehart and Winston, 1968.

Rutter, Michael et al. *Fifteen Thousand Hours.* Cambridge, Mass.: Harvard University Press, 1979.

Seers, Dudley, ed. *Cuba: The Economic and Social Revolution.* Chapel Hill: The University of North Carolina Press, 1964.

Silberman, Charles. *Crisis in the Classroom.* New York: Random House, 1970.

Steinberg, Stephen. *The Academic Melting Pot.* New Brunswick, N.J.: Transaction Books, 1977.

————. *The Ethnic Myth.* New York: Atheneum, 1981.

Steinfels, Peter. *The Neoconservatives.* New York: Simon & Schuster, 1979.

Thernstrom, Stephan. *The Other Bostonians: Poverty and Progress in the American Metropolis, 1880–1970.* Cambridge, Mass.: Harvard University Press, 1973.

————. *Poverty and Progress: Social Mobility in a 19th Century City.* Cambridge, Mass.: Harvard University Press, 1964.

Thurow, Lester. *The Zero Sum Society*. New York: Basic Books, 1980.
Wald, Karen. *Children of Che: Childcare and Education in Cuba*.
    Palo Alto, Calif.: Ramparts Press, 1978.
Warren, Donald R., ed. *History, Education and Public Policy*.
    Berkeley, Calif.: McCutchan, 1978.

Reports and Unpublished Materials

American Association of State Colleges and Universities. *Impres-
    sions of the Republic of Cuba*. Chicago, Ill.: ERIC Document
    Reproduction Service, ED 185–895, November 1979.
Blum, Virgil C., and O'Brien, Timothy. *Inner City Private Elemen-
    tary Education*. Milwaukee, Wis., 1980.
City University of New York. *CUNY Data Book*. New York: City
    University of New York, 1981.
Coleman, James et al. *Equality of Educational Opportunity*. Wash-
    ington, D.C.: U.S. Government Printing Office, 1966.
————. *Public and Private High Schools*. Chicago, Ill.: ERIC Doc-
    ument Reproduction Service, ED 197–403, March 1981.
Cordasco, Francesco, ed. *Toward Equal Educational Opportunity:
    The Report of the Committee on Equal Educational Oppor-
    tunities, U.S. Senate*. Montclair, N.J.: Montclair State Col-
    lege, AMS Press, Inc., 1974.
Eubanks, Eugene E., and Levine, Daniel U. *A First Look at Effec-
    tive School Projects at Inner City Elementary Schools*. Kan-
    sas City, Mo., 1983.
Kaufman, Barry et al. *Outcomes of Educational Opportunity: A Study
    of Graduates from City University*. New York: City Univer-
    sity Report, October 1981.
Lazar, Irving, and Darlington, Richard B. *Lasting Effects After Pre-
    school*. Ithaca, N.Y.: Cornell University, October 1978.
Levine, Daniel U., and Stark, Joyce. *Instructional and Organiza-
    tional Arrangements for Improving Achievement at Inner City
    Elementary Schools*. Kansas City, Mo., 1982.
Ministry of Education, Cuba. *Report of the Republic of Cuba to the
    38th International Conference on Public Education*. Havana,
    1981.
National Center for Education Statistics. *Digest of Education Statis-
    tics 1980*. Washington, D. C.: U. S. Government Printing Of-
    fice, 1981.
————. *Digest of Education Statistics 1982*. Washington, D.C.: U.S.
    Government Printing Office, 1983.

New York City Public Schools. *Pupil Reading Achievement.* New York: Board of Education, 1980.

Paulson, Rolland G. *Pre-Conditions for Systems-Wide Educational Reform: Learning from the Cuban Experience.* Chicago, Ill.: ERIC Document Reproduction Service, ED 128–250, April 1976.

United Nations Committee on Technology and Development. *Health and Educational Technology in Cuba.* Geneva: United Nations, August 31, 1979.

United Nations Educational, Scientific and Cultural Organization. *Methods and Means Utilized in Cuba to Eliminate Illiteracy.* Havana: Editora Pedagogica, 1965.

Weber, George. *Inner-City Children Can Be Taught to Read: Four Successful Schools.* Washington, D.C.: Council for Basic Education, 1971.

Westinghouse Learning Corporation and Ohio University. *The Impact of Head Start.* Washington, D.C.: U.S. Department of Commerce, June 1969.

Articles

Berrol, Selma C. "Education and Economic Mobility: The Jewish Experience in New York City, 1880–1920." *American Jewish Historical Quarterly* 65, no. 3 (March 1976).

Berube, Maurice R. "Education and the Poor." *Commonweal* (March 31, 1967).

———. "Head Start to Nowhere." *Commonweal* (May 30, 1969).

Bowles, Samuel. "Cuban Education and the Revolutionary Ideology." *Harvard Educational Review* 41, no. 4 (November 1971).

Center for Cuban Studies. *Cuba Update* 1, no. 6 (January 1981).

Cole, Johnnetta B. "Race Toward Equality: The Impact of the Cuban Revolution on Racism." *The Black Scholar* (November-December 1980).

Comer, James. "On Inner-City Education." *New York Times*, September 23, 1980.

Cruickshank, Donald R. "Five Areas of Teacher Concern." *Phi Delta Kappan* 63, no. 7 (March 1982).

Cuban, Larry. "Effective Schools: A Friendly but Cautionary Note." *Phi Delta Kappan* 64, no. 10 (June 1983).

Cuttace, Peter. "Reflections on the Rutter Ethos." *Urban Education* 16, no. 4 (January 1982).

Darland, Dave. "Some Complexities on Accountability." *Today's Education* (January-February 1975).

Dreyfuss, Joel. "Cuba: The Racial Dilemma." *Black Enterprise* (April 1980).

Duea, Jerry. "School Officials and the Public Hold Disparate Views on Education." *Phi Delta Kappan* 63, no. 7 (March 1982).

Edmonds, Ronald. "Some Schools Work and More Can." *Social Policy* (March-April 1979).

Gallup, George H. "The 13th Annual Gallup Poll of the Public's Attitudes Toward the Public Schools." *Phi Delta Kappan* 63, no. 1 (September 1981).

Hodgkinson, Harold L. "What's Still Right with Education?" *Phi Delta Kappan* 64, no. 4 (December 1982).

Jencks, Christopher. "Reappraisal of the Most Controversial Educational Document of Our Time," *New York Times* magazine, August 1969.

Hoyt, Robert. "Learning a Lesson from the Catholic Schools." *New York* (September 12, 1977).

Leiner, Marvin. "Two Decades of Educational Change in Cuba." *Journal of Reading* 25, no. 3 (December 1981).

Levine, Daniel U. "Concentrated Poverty and Reading Achievement." *The Urban Review* 2, no. 2 (Summer 1979).

Little, Roger. "Basic Education of Youth Socialization in the Armed Forces." *American Journal of Orthopsychiatry* 38, no. 5 (October 1968).

Maeroff, Gene I. "Reading Data Indicate Decline in Reasoning." *New York Times*, April 21, 1981.

Mujica, René J. "Some Recollections of My Experiences in the Cuban Literacy Campaign." *Journal of Reading* 25, no. 3 (December 1981).

Pollack, Cecelia, and Martuza, Victor. "Teaching Reading in the Cuban Primary Schools." *Journal of Reading* 25, no. 3 (December 1981).

Prieto, Abel. "A Conversation with Abel Prieto." *Journal of Reading* 25, no. 3 (December 1981).

————. "The Literacy Campaign in Cuba." *Harvard Educational Review* 51, no. 1 (February 1981).

Purkey, Stewart C., and Smith, Marshall S. "Too Soon to Cheer? Synthesis of Research on Effective Schools." *Educational Leadership* (December 1982).

Ralph, John A., and Fennessey, James. "Science or Reform: Some Questions About the Effective Schools Model." *Phi Delta Kappan* 64, no. 10 (June 1983).

Shanker, Albert. "Extra Effort Shows in Reading Results." *New York Times*, June 14, 1981.
————. "Teaching Is More Than Media-Hype." *New York Times*, March 7, 1982.
————. "Which Coleman Report Do We Believe?" *New York Times*, April 12, 1981.

Interviews

Arazo, Maria Elena Torrez. Principal, Valdes Rodriguez Primary School, Havana. Interview, May 10, 1983.
Fernández, José R. Minister of education, Havana. Interview, May 14, 1983.
García Elisa Wong. Deputy minister of education, Havana, Interview, May 11, 1983.
Gonzalez, Sara. Director of International Relations Section of the Ernesto "Che" Guevara Pioneer Palace, Havana. Interview, May 12, 1983.
Gutierrez, Allan. Principal, José Antonio Echeverría Intermediate School, Havana. Interview, May 12, 1983.
Jiminez, Nilda. Principal, Ejercito Rebelde Primary School, Havana. Interview, May 11, 1983.
Lopez, Merida. Researcher, Ministry of Education, Havana. Interview, May 9, 1983.
Mosot, Antonio. Director of extra school activities, Ministry of Education, Havana. Interview, May 11, 1983.
Ojeda, Magaly García. Director of primary schools, Ministry of Education, Havana. Interview, May 10, 1983.

Book Reviews

Glazer, Nathan. Review of *The Economic Basis of Ethnic Solidarity* by Edna Bonacich and John Modell, *A Piece of the Pie* by Stanley Lieberson, and *The Ethnic Myth* by Stephen Steinberg, in *The New Republic*, July 4 and 11, 1981.
Katz, Michael. Review of Diane Ravitch's *The Revisionists Revised*. *Harvard Educational Review* 49, no. 2 (May 1979).

INDEX

About the Author

MAURICE R. BERUBE is Associate Professor of Urban Education at Old Dominion University. He is the author of *The Urban University in America* (Greenwood Press, 1978), co-author of *Local Control in Education* and *School Boards and School Policy* and co-editor of *Confrontation at Ocean Hill-Brownsville*. His articles have been published in *Social Policy, Commonweal, The Nation, New Politics, Cross Currents,* and other journals.